To all those who cherish their memories of Modern School

Lala Raghubir Singh, 1895-1959

Centenary Year Edition 1920-2020

A DREAM TURNS SEVENTY FIVE

The Modern School 1920-1995

Editors

Khushwant Singh
Syeda Saiyidain Hameed

Allied Publishers Pvt. Ltd.
NEW DELHI • MUMBAI • KOLKATA
CHENNAI • BANGALORE • HYDERABAD

ALLIED PUBLISHERS PRIVATE LIMITED

Regd. Off.: 1/13-14 Asaf Ali Road, **New Delhi**–110002
Ph.: 011-23239001 • E-mail: delhi.books@alliedpublishers.com

17 Chittaranjan Avenue, **Kolkata**–700072
Ph.: 033-22129618 • E-mail: cal.books@alliedpublishers.com

15 J.N. Heredia Marg, Ballard Estate, **Mumbai**–400001
Ph.: 022-42126969 • E-mail: mumbai.books@alliedpublishers.com

No. 25/10 Commander-in-Chief Road, Ethiraj Lane (Next to Post Office) Egmore, **Chennai**–600008
Ph.: 044-28223938 • E-mail: chennai.books@alliedpublishers.com

P.B No. 9932, No. 15, 3rd Floor (Next to Vijaya Bank), 5th Cross, Gandhinagar, Karnataka, India, **Bangalore**–560009,
Ph.: 080-41530285 / 22386239 • E-mail: bngl.journals@alliedpublishers.com / apsabng@airtelmail.in

Sri Jayalakshmi Nilayam, No. 3-4-510, 3rd Floor (Above More Super Market) Barkatpura, **Hyderabad**–500027
Ph.: 040-27551811, 040-27551812 • E-mail: hyd.books@alliedpublishers.com

Website: www.alliedpublishers.com

First Published 1995
Centenary Year Edition 2020

Cover designed by Suhani Arora Sen

ISBN: 978-93-89934-20-5

Published by Sunil Sachdev and printed by Ravi Sachdev at Allied Publishers Pvt. Ltd.
1/13-14 Asaf Ali Road, New Delhi - 110002

Acknowledgements
(Centenary Edition)

The first edition of the book **A Dream Turns Seventy Five** was published in 1995 to celebrate the Platinum Jubilee of Modern School. Now, at the momentous occasion of Centenary Year celebration, we are pleased to offer you the second edition of the book. Will it not be apt to call it Nostalgia Edition!

The content remains essentially the same as it is of immense value and timeless. *A Calendar of Events* after page 62 has been updated. Photographs now consist of 32 pages instead of original 24. Immediately after that, events in the chapter *Time's Winged Chariot* have been updated to the current year, 2020, marking important events of each year. In the Appendix section, Appendix I, *Rudra Prize* has been updated till year 2019. Appendix II, *Roll of Honour*, shows pics and write-ups of five brave-hearts, who made the school proud by their heroics while defending our motherland. Finally, the last three pages about the Contributors to this book have been suitably amended.

This task could be made possible mainly because of support and whole-hearted guidance of the Board of Trustees, Author, School Authorities and Staff Members. In particular, we would like to thank Dr Syeda S. Hameed, Mr Ashok Pratap Singh, Ms Ketaki Sood, Ms Ambika Pant, Mr Sunder Hemrajani, Dr Vijay Datta and Mr Naval Singh. We thank them profusely and are grateful for their kind support.

October, 2020

Ravi Sachdev
Allied Publishers

The School Motto

नायनात्मा बलहीनेन लभ्य

The weak cannot attain self-realisation

हर धर्म के हर इक ग्रंथ ने,
हर देश के हर इक संत ने,
वीरों के हर इक वंश ने,
उपनिषद के अनुपम अंश ने,
स्पष्ट स्वरों में यही कहा
"नायमात्मा बलहीनेन लभ्यः"
बलवान बनो, बलवान बनो
पर अच्छे इक इनसान बनो ॥

— Stanza from a song written for the Platinum Jubilee by Ved Vyas and set to music by Ustad Amjad Ali Khan

The School Crest

Designed by Sarada Ukil

The School Crest signifies the circle of eternity crossed by the three elements in human development of body, mind and spirit, the sun shining between the triangle and the circle. Inside the triangle there is a banyan tree to represent stability and firmness of character, the swan and the lotus represent refinement, culture and the arts which are fundamental to human development.

— Raghubir Singh

उप - राष्ट्रपति, भारत
नई दिल्ली

VICE-PRESIDENT
INDIA
NEW DELHI

September 15, 1995

Foreword

I am glad to know that the Modern School, Delhi is celebrating its Platinum Jubilee this year.

For an educational institution to devote seventy-five years in the quest for learning is no mean achievement. Beginning with a small group of six students in 1920, it was established in the historic period of our freedom struggle and has grown over the years into one of the finest schools of our country.

The credit for its success lies in the vision and commitment of its founder, Lala Raghubir Singh. Its eventful history of seventy-five years is replete with creative and imaginative action for the cause of imparting education to the youth. Through a wide spectrum of activities, the School has rendered valuable service to the cause of education and made important contributions in widening the awareness of young students. In the pursuit of this enlightening task, this School has become a model of excellence to many others.

Its students, both past and present, have excelled in many walks of life and emerged as responsible citizens of our country. It is in schools that a sense of discipline, dedication and patriotism is nurtured. In keeping with the spirit and objectives of its creation, the Modern School has not only provided an atmosphere for academic and extra-curricular excellence but also imparted modern education to fulfil the needs of a 'borderless world'.

In an age characterised by the relentless pursuit of materialism, it is necessary to orient teaching for the creation of better 'human beings' rather than 'mental machines'. Our culture and heritage which are marked by humanism, tolerance and unity of mankind, provides a good foundation in making education socially relevant. It is imperative to have a balanced approach blending modernity with tradition.

I am confident that the School while celebrating its Platinum Jubilee and tracing its glorious past will further endeavour with redoubled vigour to enrich its contributions towards nation-building and international understanding.

Narayanan K.R.

(K.R. NARAYANAN)

Introduction

The two of us who have edited this volume, share a common experience—Modern School. Khushwant Singh, the batch of 1920, among the first six students of Modern School. Syeda Saiyidain, one among four hundred students, who joined Modern thirty years later. The preparation of this book evoked in both of us, individually and together, memories of our school days. There was no tangible thing that featured in our common recollections. We did not even have the same school building. With the exception of one, Pandit K.D.Bhardwaj, we did not have any common teachers. But in certain other ways it seemed as if time had stood still in the years that spanned our respective terms in Modern School. We were to discover, during the weeks and months of editing *A Dream Turns Seventy Five*, that the spirit of the school has remained unchanged.

It was seventy-five years ago that a man called Sobha Singh, with little formal education himself, became a partner with his younger friend Raghubir Singh in the dream of building a school which would combine the traditional with the modern educational values. I, Khushwant, was his second son, who along with my older brother, Bhagwant was enrolled on the very first day. Father was one of the most liberal men not only of his own time but for all times. It was Sardar Sujan Singh, our grandfather, who was a tough nut. Once he came to a school function at which my brother and I, along with other kindergarten children, were playing sitars in the school orchestra. He was disgusted at seeing us engaged in such 'feminine' pursuits. But when he saw Miss Bose presiding over the function, he could not contain himself and told Papaji that he should have known better than to have expected any real grit from male children whose education was entrusted to a woman! My autobiography gives some candid glimpses into my school days.

I, Syeda, thirty-five years after leaving Modern, can unabashedly say that those were the happiest four years of my life. Prior to Modern, my schooling was a subject of continued controversy between my parents. My mother preferred to see me in convents where I would be educated under the strict discipline of the nuns. Not that I was a brat, but that was her strictly feudal outlook on education. My father, himself a distinguished educationist, wanted to see me in a liberal co-educational school, specially where academic and extra-curricular activities were given equal emphasis. I recall that when we lived in Bombay, I had to attend two schools to fulfil the requirements of both parents. I attended J.B.Petit School in the forenoon and Gamadhiya School in the afternoon. That proved too much for me and ultimately even for my parents.

When I was finally transferred to Modern School in the mid-fifties, I was still hurt from an incident which today would be called a communal encounter. I say still because it had been resolved for all practical purposes and a couple of years had passed. But it continued to hover over me and I could not get it out of my mind. I want to write about this incident here because it brought into my life a man who was to become my lifelong friend. His name is Khushwant Singh. This communal encounter may have had a crippling effect if it was not for Khushwant Singh and Modern School. It happened like this.

My family came to live in Delhi in 1951. Most of our relatives had migrated to Pakistan because our ancestral town of Panipat had been emptied of all Muslims, most of whom were safely transported by government order to the other side of the Indian border. My father, under the influence of Mahatma Gandhi, Maulana Azad, Jawaharlal Nehru and Zakir Husain, decided to stay back. We children were brought up in a gently devout Muslim household and within the most liberal and enlightened traditions of Islam. In Delhi we were provided accomodation in a mixed neighbourhood consisting of old residents and newcomers from West Punjab. I started playing in the park with the neighbourhood children. One day someone asked me the question which I had learnt to dread due to my secret reading of new literature born of the Partition trauma of writers and poets. A small girl asked, 'What caste are you?' So far I had successfully avoided the issue by concealing my name but now I was caught.

When the children discovered that I was a Muslim by 'caste' they said that no one would play with me. The humiliation of having to go home and relate this to my father still makes me wince. Meanwhile, the children's grapevine sent the word around that a little Muslim girl was not to be played with. It was then that a Sikh neighbour came calling on us with his little daughter, and she became my one and only and best friend. Thus the tragedy was averted. But my father suggested that while the incident was still fresh, I write it up as a story for the children's number of the magazine, *Shankar's Weekly*. A young Argentinan artist, Brigitte Frankfurter, from Buenos Aires read my story which she found stirring. She took up her brush, illustrated it and sent it to me as a little book. The illustrations were so beautiful that the book was published by Rajkamal Prakashan. That was when I received my first 'fan' mail. The fan wrote that he had been 'moved to tears'. Since he happened to live in the same block, my father and I went up to his door and rang the doorbell. I was painfully shy. That was my first encounter with Khushwant Singh. As I was to discover later, he had just completed his two volume *History of the Sikhs* and understood the spirit of all religions better than most people. I might add that forty-five years later I am still ringing his doorbell.

It was my first day at Modern School. My father had left me in the Principal's office. Mr. Kapur took me by the hand to the morning assembly. There everyone knew one another from long association through Kindergarten and Junior schools. I stuck out—one who had dared to enter closed circles, a gawky newcomer in an out-of-uniform *shalwar-kameez*. The day seemed endless. Mr. Kapur, majestic in his black academic gown seemed omnipresent. I imagined him as my emotional anchor in the waves of blue uniforms which seemed to engulf me. The Social Hour was announced. Talent after talent flashed across the stage. I wanted to sink into the wooden floor of the gymnasium with growing awareness of my own awkwardness and some apprehension of Mr.Kapur's canny reputation for singling out individuals.

Suddenly he was calling my name. I darted a look across the hall and met his eyes. They were at once bemused and filled with kindness—exuding strength. In a flash, I recalled seeing a theatrical performance of Sir Geoffrey Kendal's 'Shakespeareana' doing *Merchant of Venice*. Between the acts there was a filler, a popular song, 'Where are you going my pretty maid?' rendered by two players. I had been struck with the sauciness of the girl who acted the part of the cockney milkmaid. In a few seconds I was playing both roles, the maid and her beau, and taking my bows to a thunderous applause. Once again, I was intensely aware of Mr.Kapur's unspoken *shabaash*.

It was his unbounded kindness and the healing ambience of Modern School, gathered into a few moments of performance at the gymnasium, that ultimately wiped the echo of the words 'What is your caste?' Recalling the lines spoken by Edgar in Shakespeare's immortal tragedy,*King Lear*—

Men must abide their going hence
Even as their coming thither
Ripeness is all

I realised that in Modern School excellence was all. That was the creed of Lala Raghubir Singh and Mr. M.N.Kapur. Those four years gave me a sense of dignity and self worth. I never lost it despite the somewhat rough terrain of subsequent years and the general hardening of communal feelings all around the world, wherever I lived.

This volume which commemorates seventy-five years of Modern School is divided in two sections; we have called the first section *The Inspiration*, the second *The Memory*. In the first, we have explored the genesis of Modern School. Using the private archives of the Raghubir Singh family, we have tried to discover how the idea was born. Among the carefully preserved correspondence we found a valuable source—letters written by Sultan Singh to his son Raghubir. In them, the father discussed, advised and helped his son realise his dream of establishing a school. From Sultan Singh's letters we were able to construct the likely replies of Raghubir

Singh and the pieces of the story started to fit. We also relied on oral history. From members of the family we gathered pieces of precious history. We learnt that Sushila Sultan Singh was a pioneer of women's education and her school for the purdah girls of the inner city still exists in Daryaganj. We gathered that Modern School Daryaganj was across the road from Dr.M.A.Ansari's house which at the time of the school's inception was the hub of political activities. Talking to the first batch of students, we discovered how the school spirit, which is what Modern is all about, was first engendered among the boys and girls. We found out that then, as now, the girls played all the games with the boys—football, cricket, hockey. Whether riding horses or climbing trees they were neck to neck in every activity.

We learnt that the first class of three who matriculated in 1928 called themselves 'The Three Musketeers'. They were Bhagwant Singh, Anant Singh and Rajeshwar Batra. Sixty-seven years later, in 1995, Bhagwant and Anant are at the top of the pyramid—at the apex of the Modernites who are now tens of thousands, spread over all parts of the world. Rajeshwar became a pilot and was killed in 1937 in an air crash. The first section thus features all those who spun the dream, the inspired men and women who made Modern School what it is today. From Sultan Singh, elegant gentleman and a great visionary, who owned almost all the property in Kashmiri Gate and shopped in Europe for his wardrobe, to C.F.Andrews, who could not even bring himself to owning a single decent set of clothes, they were bound together in a common pursuit. They all are represented in some fashion or another in the first section of the book.

Wedged between the two parts is a section 'Time's Wingéd Chariot' the title of which is taken from a poem of Andrew Marvel. It covers the major events of the seventy-five years. This is not meant as a calendar of events, a catalogue of achievements or a listing of the dignitaries who visited Modern Scchool. The editors have selected for inclusion, a few landmark events which have shaped the school. Certain criteria were used as the basis for inclusion but a subjective judgement could not entirely be avoided.

The second part is called 'The Memory'. Drawing upon the experiences of a few Modernites, we have tried to construct a section which covers every aspect of the school. We have started with the oldest and ended with the youngest Modernite—from Bhagwant Singh who matriculated in 1928, to Alieda Ali Baig who will finish school in 1996. The two aspects of school life, the academic and the extra-curricular are the subjects of the various articles. How was the balance created between the two aspects? What was the relationship between the teachers and students? How did the girls feel as an overwhelming minority? What was the state of the fine and performing arts education? Art, music, dance, drama, all appear in multi-layered interpretations by people who today are renowned practitioners in the various fields, the seedlings of which were planted and nurtured in Modern School.

Himself an accomplished sportsman, specially swimming and boxing, Mr.Kapur wanted every student to play some sport and above all imbibe the sportsman's spirit. The philosophy of sports, method of reward and punishment, education through travel, life in the hostel, House system, community service, all facets find a place in the second section. Finally, there are projections into the future in the form of visions for the Modern Schools—Barakhamba Road, Humayun Road, and Vasant Vihar in the 21st century. Perhaps some aspects merited a closer look and a detailed treatment but we were not always able to make people adhere to their promises of writing for us.

As for us, we have enjoyed working together on this book. It has given us an opportunity of renewing some old and cherished friendships. There is something so special about sharing school memories that we were able to recreate a bond with whomsoever we approached in this regard. As editors of this volume we would like to take this opportunity of thanking most warmly all those who responded so readily to our invitation to contribute to this special commemorative publication. We are grateful to all the people from whose recollections we constructed the oral history of the school. To the Raghubir Singh family we want to express our deep appreciation, especially General Virendra Singh, Ashok Pratap Singh and Anju Pratap Singh. We received invaluable help from Mrs.Amrita Kapur, and many excellent suggestions from Geeta Kapur. We are grateful to Mr.O.P.Sharma without whose generous sharing of his time and his sources this book could not have been produced. We are thankful to Allied Publishers, particularly Ravi Sachdeva. Our gratitude to Surojit Banerjee for his expert assistance with the publication.

Khushwant Singh
Syeda Saiyidain Hameed

21 October, 1995

Contents

THE MEMORY

APPENDICES

The Inspiration

We are the music makers,
We are the dreamers of dreams

—From an Ode by Arthur O'Shaughnessy

The Dreamer And His Dream

Khushwant Singh

Every great project begins with a dream. The dreamer becomes obsessed with his dream and pursues it relentlessly. He tells his friends and relatives about it and persuades them to join him in making his dream become a reality. This story is about one such dreamer, Raghubir Singh—and his dream of setting up an institution combining the best of ancient Indian tradition with the needs of the times. He spent his entire life in the fulfilment of that dream.

First a few words about Raghubir Singh's ancestry and family background. His grandfather, Nihal Singh, was from a Rajput family whose forefathers had abandoned Rajput martial traditions, converted to Jainism and settled to more peaceful occupations of banking and commerce in Delhi. Nihal Singh had two sons, Multan Singh and Sultan Singh. Multan Singh had no children. Sultan Singh had a son (Raghubir Singh) and a daughter. Multan Singh died suddenly. Rather than introducing a stranger in the family, Sultan Singh agreed to give his only son, Raghubir Singh, in adoption to his newly widowed sister-in-law. The adoption ceremony took place during the period of mourning. Without any prior warning, three-year old Raghubir Singh was placed in the lap of his widowed aunt. This was in the year 1898.

A few years later, Sultan Singh's own wife died and he took a second wife, Sushila, daughter of a businessman from Saharanpur. Thus Raghubir Singh, having lost his own mother, had two surrogate mothers, one his aunt who had adopted him and who he addressed as Ammaji, and the other his stepmother who he called Bari Bhaboji.

Sultan Singh's primary business was that of an accountant (*khazanchi*) and treasurer of the Imperial Bank of India. Besides holding cash for the bank, he handled all its commercial transactions. His credit was high both with the British rulers and the Indian princes. The properties in Kashmiri Gate which he eventually developed were known as Sikander Bagh and were purchased by the Deputy Commissioner of Delhi when Sultan Singh's and his brother Multan Singh's properties and other assets were in the Court of Wards. These estates originally belonged to the Anglo-Indian soldier of fortune, Colonel James Skinner of Skinner's Horse, who built

St. James' Church and joined it with a small park and a beautiful mosque for the use of his many Muslim wives. In the orchard Col. James Skinner had built his billiard room; there was also a beautiful *chhatri* (canopy). There Sultan Singh developed his property and built his own residence, guest houses and servant quarters.

Sultan Singh was a man of taste and a *bon vivant*. He went to Europe twice, taking with him his wife, his valet and cook. For himself, he brought the most expensive ties from Paris, and fancy luggage from the most expensive luggage makers, Louis Viton. He hired a governess to teach Sushila English. She never tired of telling her great-grandchildren of her adventures in Europe.

Some financial matters were to cause concern to Sultan Singh. A man by the name of R.E. Grant Govern started the Clive Motor Works. Sultan Singh stood surety for a large loan taken by the company from the Central Bank of India. There were some debts for his son to clear after he was gone. The son was not interested in commerce or banking because his interests lay elsewhere. Many years before his father's death in 1930, he had embarked on the project nearest to his heart—to set up the best school in Northern India. He had the full support of his father who gave him a large sprawling mansion with extensive grounds in Daryaganj for the purpose. He also persuaded his Sikh friend Sobha Singh, recently arrived in Delhi to participate in the construction of the new capital, to join them in the venture.

Neither Sobha Singh nor Sultan Singh had much education. Sobha Singh had only studied up to the matriculation class at the Khalsa College, Amritsar. He did not sit for the exam and joined his father, Sujan Singh in the construction business. He hired a Maharashtrian teacher to teach him English. Nevertheless, he went along with Sultan Singh and entered his two elder sons in Raghubir Singh's school. He was to stand by Raghubir Singh all through his life.

What were the childhood influences which moulded Raghubir Singh's life? Who were the men and women who moulded his dreams? He was born in a Digamber Jain family, but his father Sultan Singh, though involved with several Jain institutions, was a broadminded man who had seen a lot of the world and made close friends with men of other communities, Muslims, Sikhs and Christians, both Indian and foreign. Among his Muslim friends was Dr. M.A. Ansari, fast rising as a nationalist politician, and among the Sikhs was the young builder Sobha Singh who built a large house on Prithviraj Road for Raghubir. Then there was the young English parson C.F. Andrews, who had joined the staff of St. Stephen's College, opened by the Cambridge Mission in Kashmiri Gate. Sultan Singh was very much taken up by Andrews' commitment to poverty. Andrews wore old clothes, often in tatters. Sultan Singh had him measured by Delhi's leading English tailors, Phelps and Rankin, and fitted out in smart European suits. It didn't take long for Andrews to give away the expensive clothes gifted to him and don his loose fitting soiled garments. It was to Andrews that Sultan turned to for advice for getting an English tutor for his son. Andrews recommended a friend Willy Pearson, who he had known from the time they had worked with Mahatma Gandhi in South Africa. Pearson spent two years in Sultan Singh's home coaching Raghubir Singh.

There was much coming and going of politicians in Sultan Singh's home in Kashmiri Gate. Though given the title of Rai Bahadur with a Kaiser-e-Hind gold medal by the British government and a banker looking after state accounts, Sultan Singh kept an open house for national leaders. Mahatma Gandhi, always stayed with him whenever he was in Delhi. Young Raghubir often played host to him when his father was away and became very friendly with Gandhi's personal secretary, Mahadev Desai.

Sultan Singh had hoped that his son would take over his banking business and management of real estate. He had by then bought more property which once belonged to James Skinner in Kashmiri Gate. He owned shops in Chandni Chowk, houses in Kashmiri Gate and Subzi Mandi. He arranged Raghubir's marriage to Premvati, daughter of a prosperous Jain family of Pahari Dhiraj near Sadar Bazar, engaged in brocade (*guota*) business. The marriage took place in 1913. Premvati bore Raghubir three children, Pratap Singh (b. 1915), Virendra Singh (b. 1917) and Rita (b. 1919). Thereafter Premvati's health began to deteriorate. For long periods she was confined to bed or the wheelchair and could only take a few steps helped by someone. Raghubir Singh had to nurse his wife and look after his three children. Once when Gandhiji was staying with them, he helped Premvati with his nature-cure methods.

Raghubir Singh went to school in a government run institution in Mori Gate. It was during his years at school that he came to know Master Amir Chand, who unknown to him was a member of a revolutionary group led by Rash Bihari Bose. They planned the assassination of Viceroy Lord Hardinge when he came to Delhi to inaugurate the Coronation Durbar. As the procession was passing through Chandni Chowk, a bomb was hurled from the roof of a building on the elephant on which the Viceroy and Vicerene were riding. The umbrella bearer was killed instantly and the Viceroy was seriously injured. Rash Bihari Bose escaped to Japan. Master Amir Chand was not so lucky. He was arrested, tried with co-conspirators and hanged. This left a deep impression on the mind of young Raghubir Singh who now looked upon Amir Chand as a hero.

Sultan Singh was a very caring father, and undoubtedly a dominant if not domineering influence on his children. He continued performing his duties as the first citizen of Delhi, as Chairman of the city's Municipal Corporation, as founder-chairman of Delhi Cloth Mills, also various charitable institutions. At the same time he persevered in his generous hospitality. Besides Gandhi and his disciples, he threw open his house to the Maharajas of Kashmir and Mysore and their families.

Despite enjoying patronage of the government, he used to attend the annual Congress session. In 1917 he attended the Congress session in Lucknow and persuaded the nationalist leaders to hold the next session in Delhi. He raised funds to make the Delhi session a grand success. When the government expressed disapproval of his activities he surrendered his title and the Kaiser-i-Hind medal.

It is not difficult to visualise the atmosphere in which young Raghubir Singh was reared, It was a mixture of the traditional Indian and modern European education, a striving for freedom without abandoning norms held sacred by Indians, the central point of the Jain faith—*Ahimsa*, non-violence in thought and in deed. It was vibrant Gandhism enshrined in his two favourite hymns;

Vaishnav jan to taine kahiyee
Je peerh paraiee jane ray

Call only him a man of faith
Who senses the anguish in another's heart

and

Ishwar Allah tere nam
Sab ko sanmati dey Bhagwan.

Ishwar and Allah are both thy names;
May God's grace descend on everyone.

Sultan Singh realised that his son was not interested in business or politics. He had set his sights on higher things—to nurture a generation of Indian boys and girls who would be at once dedicated to their past and yet be modern in their outlook. Once the realization dawned on him, he lent his son his full support. Besides putting his large sprawling mansion owned in Daryaganj, facing the house of his friend M.A. Ansari, at his disposal, he provided him funds to get the institution going. He was abroad when his son opened the school. He sent a donation of Rs. 5000 (a very big sum for those days). When he returned to Delhi, he persuaded many friends to join the school society. They included engineers like Rai Bahadur Devi Singh and Teja Singh Malik (later knighted), building contractors Baisakha Singh and Narain Singh. And above others Sobha Singh (also later knighted), whose association continued to the end of his days.

Sultan Singh led a life full of multifarious activities. In 1929, he was in Europe buying furniture and equipment for his new house. He returned to Delhi to resume his routine of work and entertainment. One morning he went to preside over a meeting of Delhi Cloth Mills (DCM had its head office at Bara Hindu Rao). When he returned home he fell sick. Dr. Ansari diagnosed it was dyptheria. Two days later on the evening of June 3 1930, he died peacefully.

We go back a few years to mention the name of a lady who was to play a decisive role in giving shape to Raghubir Singh's vision of the future. He was on the lookout for someone who would head his institution. He met Kamala Bose, a Bengali Christian, who had migrated from Calcutta to Delhi to take over as companion and tutor to Rai Bahadur Narain Singh's daughter, Balwant Kaur, whose husband had deserted her after she had a son, Mohinder Singh. At their very first meeting Raghubir Singh sensed that Kamala Bose was exactly the sort of person he was looking for and invited her to become the Principal of his school. She accepted the invitation without any hesitation. Thus in 1920 was born Modern School. Its first students were Raghubir Singh's three children. Soon thereafter, Teja Singh's son and daughter, Devi Singh's two sons and Sobha Singh's two boys were also enrolled.

Letters From Father To Son

Syeda Saiyidain Hameed

The genesis of the Modern School precedes by several years its formal opening on 20 October, 1920. The idea was first planted in the mind of a man called Raghubir Singh by his father, Rai Bahadur Lala Sultan Singh. Evidence of this is available in the correspondence between the father and son, the earliest of which was written on 20 April 1912. This is how it happened.

At one o'clock in the afternoon of 20 April, three men boarded *S.S. Mantua* from Bombay on their way to London via Aden, Port Said and Marseilles. They were Sushil Kumar Rudra, Principal of St. Stephen's College, Reverend C.F. Andrews, a member of the teaching staff of St. Stephen's and a friend of Mahatma Gandhi and Rabindranath Tagore, and Sultan Singh, a prominent banker and businessman of Delhi. Sultan Singh, with a heavy heart, was leaving behind his only son Raghubir for the first time. He had entrusted to the seventeen-year old boy, the care of his own elderly mother, his older brother's widow, his own wife and his vast business interests in the city of Delhi. He wrote a letter to his son the moment he got on board:

> Don't be afraid to write to me your own thoughts about any particular matter. You should now be quite free and frank with me, otherwise how shall I be able to mould you and guide your ideas? Consider me your friend first and father afterwards and not as one from whom you have to hide anything.

The letter was brought to him on shore.

The three friends, separately and together, spent six months touring England. Letters from the father to the son kept arriving from every stop on their journey; his gentle guidance continued unabated. This was the year when Raghubir had completed his matriculation and was preparing to enter college. In consultation with his two friends, both educationists, Sultan Singh decided that a person should be engaged for his son to 'undertake tutorial work' and help him prepare for college. C.F. Andrews came up with the name of a person who he considered to be most suitable, a man called W. Winstanley Pearson, who was to have profound influence on young Raghubir. He wrote:

> My friend Willie Pearson had been sent home ill with rheumatism and lumbago from Bhowanipore, Calcutta. His health was far from good, but it seemed to all of us that the light tutorial work in a dry and sunny climate, during the cold weather at Delhi might be more invigorating than any immediate return to Calcutta. (*Modern Review*, February 1935)

The father wrote to his son that he would attend college 'as a regular college student but will have special lessons at home'. Pearson happily agreed to become the young man's tutor and return to the country he had grown to love. On 16 July 1912, he wrote the first of many letters that he was to write to his pupil:

> You will have learnt from your father that I have been appointed your private tutor and am coming to Delhi with him in October.

He sent Raghubir a photograph of himself and asked for one in return since they should recognise one another when they met for the first time. The tutor and ward corresponded regularly during these three months and came to know and respect one another even before they had actually met.

During the one year of their association, from 1913-1914, Willie Pearson's influence on Raghubir was next only to the influence of his own father. During the summer of 1913, both were sent to the mountains, away from the blistering heat of Delhi. A strict routine of study and physical exercise was followed and closely monitored by the father. Still frail from his earlier ailments, although much better than before, Pearson was tenderly looked after by his pupil. His father wrote from his Eden Cottage in Simla:

> Make Mr. Pearson comfortable. Do not forget for a moment that you cannot buy knowledge, it is a gift from the teacher and the pupil must receive it with humility and gratitude. (21 June 1913)

No effort was spared when Willie fell ill during the tutorial holiday. Father firmly directed the son to spare no expense and personally care for his diet, his medicine and doctor. The teacher was the gateway to a noble life. He wrote from Delhi on 19 August 1913:

> I wish you would try and understand your duties towards elders, teachers, and your other fellow beings in their true proportion and aspire to make your life one of service and usefulness. If you talk on these subjects with Mr. Pearson and take his example to heart, I assure you that you will be much benefited. It is a golden opportunity and your good fortune that you have had such a good man to teach you, but it rests with you to take full advantage of it. Money cannot buy knowledge nor any right conduct, it is reverence to the Guru and

one's own discipline which contributes to one's real advancement.

Sultan Singh's faith in the teacher was more than justified. Pearson reinforced the high ideals that had been ingrained in his pupil. He was himself grounded in the Indian ethos and steeped in the ancient values of the East. Consequently, he took pleasure in moulding the eager and receptive mind of his pupil. A month after the advice from his father, Raghubir received a letter from his tutor which he wrote from a camp at Kot, after a hard day's trek from Simla to Kulu, in the company of his employer Sultan Singh; the letter was written by the light of a lantern.

> The Manager of the timber works lent me a copy of one volume of *The Mahabharata* to read and I have been reading it this evening. I was struck by the following passage which seems to me to throw some light on one or two conversations we had up in Mussourie; and as it is from your own religious book it will perhaps be more impressive to you than any amount of advice. The passage runs thus: 'Those families, O Bharata, that are possessed of members, wealth and kine, are not regarded as families if they be wanting in good manners and conduct, while families wanting in wealth but distinguished by manners and good conduct are regarded as such and win great reputation. *Therefore should good manners and conduct be cherished with care, for as regards wealth it cometh and goeth.* He that is wanting in wealth is not really wanting, but he that is wanting in manners and conduct is really wanting.' Remember what I said about the root of good manners being in thinking of others rather than oneself. So cherish good manners and conduct so you may always possess that which can never be lost. (30 September 1913)

In the sprawling *haveli* of Sultan Singh, Raghubir was growing up under his father's care and vigilant eye. In all matters pertaining to education there was Master Amir Chand to consult with—a man highly educated, enlightened and resourceful. He was the one under whose 'loving care' Sultan Singh had entrusted, 'what is dearest to me in the world and in whom all my future hopes lie', when he had left on his first voyage to England (letter dated 20 April 1912). Master Sahib was responsible for arranging that Pandit Madho Narain taught Raghubir Urdu and Persian, and Avadh Behari taught him mathematics. On definite instructions from Sultan Singh, he was also to ensure that Panditji gave extra Urdu lessons to his wife Sushila. He was the one who had engaged Mrs. Chatterjee, a Christian lady, to tutor Sushila in English. The influence of this highly trusted and respected teacher on Raghubir was, however, not confined to purely academic matters.

There was another aspect of Master Amir Chand which shook the foundations of the British Empire. On 23 December 1912, when the Governor-General's procession was passing through Chandni Chowk, a bomb was hurled at the elephant on which Lord and Lady Hardinge were riding. The umbrella bearer was instantly killed and the Viceroy sustained a head injury. No one could trace the 'assailants'. Fourteen months later four people were arrested in connection with the Hardinge Bomb Case—Masters Amir Chand, Avadh Behari and Bal Mukund, and one Basant Kumar Biswas. Amir Chand and his companions were tried, convicted and hanged in the Delhi Central Jail on 8 May 1915. This aspect of Amir Chand is not mentioned in any of the available correspondence. But it is unlikely that much that was happening behind the closed doors of Master Amir Chand's rooms could have escaped the curiosity of a seventeen year old boy. The influence of a freedom fighter and martyr must have left a deep mark and the patriotic underpinnings of Modern School may have had their origin here.

Watching his father's determination to educate his wife (by engaging the services of teachers like Amir Chand), despite opposition from the older ladies of the household, Raghubir realised the importance of women's education. Sultan Singh spared no opportunity to impress upon the boy the need to foster education among women. On 10 May 1912, he wrote from London about three young 'Swetambara-Shrimal Jain girls' from Ahmedabad, aged fifteen, seventeen and nineteen who were staying at his boarding house and were in England for higher education. He wrote that he was struck by the fact that they had not become Europeanised or lost their individualities as Indians or Jains, while pursuing professional education.

> I wish our present day backward women may see some of this life and may feel an incentive to get rid of their ignorance. Please discuss this matter with Lala Amir Chand and let me know candidly your impressions. Don't mind if they don't agree with my views. I only wish to set you thinking.

The gender question was raised again and again in the letters, impressing the need to educate and enlighten Indian women:

> I see the women here who are as clever and enlightened as men, nay they can better take care of the household than men. Talk about this matter with Masterji (Amir Chand) and then write me an essay telling me what should be done to improve the Hindu women so that they may be able to hold their own and be not dependent on men for every little thing—like young children. (London, 7 June 1912)

The letters are replete with references to education which seems to be the overwhelming *raison d'être* for this journey. The father is exploring all the likely places where the son could go for higher studies. Although there is no specific reference in these letters to the establishment of a school, it seems as if, by their emphasis on education, they are in fact laying its foundations. On 24 May 1912, after a tour of Cambridge University, where 'there are about twenty first-class colleges' he writes:

> The sons of rich people mostly come to the university (Cambridge) as it is rather expensive and it is they who take the most prominent part in the affairs of the British Empire. They are not lie our rich people who say, *Parh kar kya karna hai. Koi naukri thori karni hai*! (What is the use of studying...one never has to seek employment)

The tutorials with Pearson lasted a year but the friendship lasted a lifetime. After completing the year, Pearson went to Bolpur and lived there with Rabindranath Tagore and C.F. Andrews, among the fraternity of Santiniketan. 'Thus Bengal gave Willie Pearson to Delhi for a short season and out of that visit many important things happened', Andrews was to write twenty years later in the *Modern Review.* That year Pearson accompanied Andrews to South Africa to help Mahatma Gandhi's mission. These men with their strong social commitment were part of Raghubir's daily life. It is not surprising that the influence of Tagore and his school is apparent in all aspects of Modern School during its first few decades. From Bolpur on 27 July 1914 Pearson congratulated his former pupil on his success in the Intermediate exam:

> I never had any doubt as to your success myself, but examinations are often trials of luck rather than tests of ability, especially in Indian universities where there are so many examinees, and therefore it is a relief to know for certain that the examiners have not made a mistake.

The next six years were a period of serious apprenticeship, during which Raghubir learnt about the responsibilities of his father's banking and other business interests. The letters of this period from the father to the son reflect the meticulous care with which he initiated him into a life where study, sports, fine arts would be balanced by a sense of responsibility for family affairs, including the intricacies of running a complex and diversified business. The idea of establishing a school began to take shape in Raghubir's mind partly as a consequence of the birth of his own son in 1915, and partly due to the growing national sentiment which neccesitated a different educational philosophy than what prevailed under the British.

In 1917, he took the first concrete step towards this goal by undertaking an educational tour. He carefully planned his visit to various educational institutions, the most important being 'The Bolpur school of Sir R.N. Tagore.' The impressions he gathered during this rather extensive tour are preserved in a rough undated diary, which he may have wanted to refine later. The fact that as early as 1917, he had discussed his project with Tagore, who was not yet a close friend, leaves no doubt that he must have thrashed it out with his tutors, particularly with Pearson, and had certainly obtained the approval of his father as the first step:

> The poet said that he was very pleased to hear about our proposed institution. It should be away from the city. A great improvement if free from the pest of examinations. A proper provision must be made for the arts.

This establishes the date of the influence of Santiniketan on Modern School, particularly in the fine and the performing arts. Other aspects of life at Bolpur also left a lasting impression on Raghubir. His account of a theatrical performance of Tagore's 'Post Office' captures a moment in history:

> R.N. Tagore was acting .... He was most wonderful. G.N. Tagore was acting as Madhav and A.N. Tagore as physician and Headman. Mr. Asit K. Haldar as curd-seller. The poet sang two songs....The play was held in 'Bichitra', a place in Tagore's house which was dedicated to public use.

When the Modern School Society was registered in August 1920, Sultan Singh was away on an extended trip to Europe. He was exploring the institutions which his son could attend for higher education and training in pedagogy. Interest in a subject, he contended, was a good start but it had to be augmented by a systematic study leading to a degree. On 21 October 1920 he wrote from England:

> I want you to take a degree in pedagogy too in this country (England) so that your voice and opinion may command more respect from the government of India than other people in whose hands will lie the shaping of the policy of education of our country. I desire that apart from carrying on and organizing your newly started school, you may acquire such knowledge of the theory and other sides of educational subjects, that you may be helpful in shaping the general policy of education in India.

The letters from London, all written during the initial days of Modern School, reflect Sultan Singh's deep commitment to his son's project. Later, he would enlist the help of all his business associates and friends in funding various capital projects for the school. Those whom he held very close, like Sardar Sobha Singh, would become part and parcel of the school, honouring his commitment to it as long as he lived. Responding to the news about formation of the Modern School Society, Sultan Singh wrote on 13 August 1920:

> I was extremely interested in the formation of 'The Modern School'. I wish the scheme all success. You have done well in promising Rs. 5000 and giving Daryaganj House rent free for three years. It has my hearty approval and I congratulate you on the idea.

The letters from father to son, in themselves, are an education. He uses every opportunity to show Raghubir a wider perspective on life. How to maximise work output, how to work with different points of view, how to delegate work:

> I am glad your school has started work from Ist September. I am quite happy to do anything you wish me to do for the success of the school. Please take one advice from me and you will find it useful. Do all that you can for the newly started institution to make it a success, but don't take the entire responsibility on your shoulders alone... I am certain you will prosper and succeed in all that you will undertake. I am sure of your honesty of purpose, sense of resonsibility and high ideals you aspire to and it makes me proud of you day by day. Actual experience of men and matters is in what you lack. You will gain in this too as time goes along, but your loving father's advice and co-operation will make up even for that and I assure you of both of these to the best of my ability. (London, 7 September 1920)

A sound financial management he believed was the best foundation for a fledgling institution. Sitting thousands of miles away in the Isle of Wight, Sultan Singh was thinking about ways and means of ensuring that the school remained financially secure during its initial period. On 27 October 1920 he wrote:

> In this world of hard facts, sentiment will not do. I hope you have collected funds and put them in the bank to carry on the school for three years, so every month you as secretary may have no bother of demanding from donors their amount.

Ever willing to try new experiments, Raghubir asked his father to look for a kindergarten teacher in England, who could be employed immediately. But members of the management committee demurred. Crestfallen, Raghubir sent a telegram asking his father to stop the search. Father's reply was a lesson in subordinating individual will in deference to group consensus:

> Regarding the telegram for the kindergarten mistress, it is alright. In an institution one has to work with the opinion of his fellow-workers and committee, and you have done quite well to cancel the requisition until all of them agree with your proposal... I am glad this starting of school will give you a lot of practical experience and will shake off from your mind many things which are found in theory but not workable in practice. You shall get knowledge of men and the world also. (London, 11 November 1920)

Visits and correspondence with Pearson continued during the initial years of Modern School. He wrote to his favourite pupil from Santiniketan as well as from his trips to places like Fiji Islands where he had gone with C.F. Andrews to study the problem of indentured labour. On 4 October 1921, he wrote from Bolpur:

> Hoping that you have got some new entries for the school and that all goes well there, including Miss Scott.

Another letter written a month later is an appeal for relief in North Bengal where flood and famine had devastated the population:

> I want you to help me in a plan I have of distributing relief in North Bengal... I propose to go in the middle of January and want to be able to take some substantial help with me in the way of clothing and as I feel specially for the children, I intend to buy *khaddar* cloth for boys and girls which I can distribute personally during my tour. I therefore want you to collect through the children of your school (and in other ways if you can) as large a sum as possible which I can spend in this way... I think such a project is likely to appeal to the children of your school, and if you yourself were able to acompany me on this visit, it would be all the better. (Santiniketan, 2 November 1921).

It appears from subsequent correspondence that Pearson could not raise any funds for this cause but the fact that he appealed to Modern School and its founder reflects his faith that the spirit of public service was engendered in the school from its very inception. This is the last piece of correspondence from Pearson. Two years later, he died in a railway accident which was reported to Raghubir Singh by telegram by C.F. Andrews, the man who had brought them together in the first place:

> Pearson died September 24, 1923 railway accident.
> Unspeakable loss. Andrews, Santiniketan.

The details followed in a letter dated 10 October 1923:

> He said to the nurse one night, 'India, my one and only love'. Those were very precious and beautiful words and they were exactly true.

Besides Sultan Singh, Pearson and Andrews, there were several others like Sobha Singh, Teja Singh who put their strength behind the school. Some of them were Raghubir's seniors, like his college Principal S.K. Rudra, after whom he was to name the most prestigious prize offered by the school. Rudra wrote that he was prepared to go on a 'begging expedition' for the school. But he hastened to add that education cannot be a commercial undertaking:

> I told you that to run a school on proper lines, efficiently and permanently, you need a permanent endowment. Education on a sound and permanent basis can never be a commercial undertaking and on strict business lines. It must be based on gifts of the wealthy-for the good and general welfare of the people of a particular class....I must caution you never to be disheartened. But

> you must go on and build up a permanent endowment by degrees and you will succeed. (Dalhousie, 5 July 1923)

Later he was to write from his deathbed at Solon where he was attended by his son Sudhir and C.F. Andrews, and watched with great concern from a distance by Raghubir Singh, about the importance of the school mission:

> You have begun a good work in the city of Delhi. Your life means so much to that city and that accounts for my concern, apart from all my personal interest in you and yours. You must take care of yourself my boy; as life is a great responsibility. (Solan, Simla Hills, 31 May 1925)

Some of the correspondence that has survived and preserved in the Raghubir Singh papers is from the first members of the staff of Modern School. It reflects the close knit group of the school fraternity. The two English women Miriam Young and Beatrice Budden, wrote to Raghubir Singh during their sojourn in England. Raihana Tyabji, daughter of Abbas Tyabji, Mahatma Gandhi's close associate, who taught music at the school for a brief period, wrote breezy chatty letters from Baroda. The common theme in the letters is how much they all missed being away from school. Budden writes:

> Here I am constantly thinking of you and the school... .I am going to put in some solid work on the teaching of English to beginners. In spite of all the various interests we, all the four of us [Budden and Young, and two girls, Dhira and Jiwani] feel homesick at times and our thoughts travel to Delhi many times a day. (Birmingham 16 May 1928)

Miriam Young worked in the school for fifteen years. In her preface to her book *Seen and Heard in a Punjab Village* which was published in 1931, she writes that during those years she was, 'More or less shut away behind the metaphorical walls of an institution which was a little world of its own and absorbed all one's time and energy, On 22 August 1928 she wrote to Raghubir Singh from Essex regarding suitable accommodation when she returned to Delhi:

> I had a letter from Miss Bose this week in which she said she had asked Mr. Ukil Babuji to look out for a suitable suite of rooms for us. If they have found anything really suitable, I should go straight there, if not and I could hear from you at Colombo that I could have rooms in the Chhatta Pratap Singh house... I am feeling exceedingly fit and greatly looking forward to taking up work again.... I am glad you have been able to buy the land in New Delhi at a reasonable rate.

After a brief spell at Modern School where she taught music, Raihana had to return to Baroda to be near her father and Gandhiji at Sevagram. Her letters reflect her admiration for the work of the Gandhians, desire to be part of it and her longing for Modern School:

> How is dear Miss Bose? I have heard from Beatrice and written to Nilima. By the way how is Babu Bala Prasadji?... .And Ukilji and Panditji?.. They have become just like my own through affection. I shall never forget their kindness to me nor yours, my brother. (Baroda Camp, 16 May 1928)

Her affection for the students is reflected in a letter in which she narrates a dream. That her feelings were fully reciprocated by her students, is evident in the account of Bharat Ram (Class of 1931) who recalls leaving his house very early every morning and cycling down so that he could stop outside her rooms in Kashmiri Gate on his way to the school and hear her sing. Raihana writes to Raghubir:

> I had such a vivid dream about you early this morning. I dreamt you had brought a whole lot of my kiddies to Baroda—Jamshed and Feroze and Gajraj and the rest. And they sung to me a beautiful song taught to them by Panditji....It is strange how those children tug at my heart. I saw them so clearly that the air seems peopled with them now and their voices ring clearly in my ears. I am in Delhi once again. (Baroda Camp, 28 July 1928.)

These letters naturally evoke the atmosphere of those early days when from a barely formulated idea in the minds of a few men, Modern School became a reality. They are a clear statement of the ideals upon which the school was grounded. The father and son team, the teachers and mentors, the patriots—both English and Indian—and the dedicated little team of experts who set the scheme in motion, all were fired by a spirit which cannot be defined in words. For a student of history, no less than a student of the school, this bunch of old letters, so carefully preserved in the family archives, are the most invaluable part of the genesis of Modern School.

Other Schools When Modern Was Born

Syeda Saiyidain Hameed

'Education is no exotic implant in India. There is no country where the love of learning had so early an origin or has exercised so lasting and powerful an influence', wrote F.W. Thomas in 1891, in *The History and Prospects of British Education in India*. A telescopic view of our ancient and medieval concept of education reveals inscriptions on stone and copper, palm leaf manuscripts of temple archives and later, after paper was manufactured, pages upon pages of printed material. The knowledge, which has thus been preserved, is unrivalled in its antiquity and the intellectual subtlety of its contents by anything which has been produced by any other civilization of the world.

After settling down in the Indo-Gangetic plains, the Aryan tribes organised themselves into four classes according to the tasks required for the functioning of society. Those designated pastors and teachers were called Brahmins, those who fought for the protection of society came to be known as Kshatriyas, those who tilled and harvested the land and sold the produce were named Vaishyas, and those who performed menial jobs became the Shudras. Thus the responsibility for imparting education remained the monopoly of the Brahmins. Life of an individual was mapped into four periods or 'ashrams'. *Brahmacharya* (student life), *Grahastashram* (married life), *Vanprasthashram* (retirement), and *Sannyas* (renunciation). The first period ran from five to eighteen years, during which the student was expected to dedicate himself entirely to his studies. To remain free from all worldly distractions, the life of celibacy was enjoined, hence the word *Brahmacharya* for studenthood.

It was maintained that a child's education in fact started at the foetal stage; the education of the mother was regarded as important as that of the offspring. Various religious ceremonies were prescribed with a view to ensuring the health of the unborn child. Education was given at home from the age of five to eight, eleven or twelve, depending on whether the child was Brahmin, Kshatriya or Vaishya. Shudras were left out of the pale of education.

The child was placed under the care of a teacher after the *Maunjibandhan* (tying of the girdle made of *munja* grass) ceremony. He was expected to live with the teather as a member of his family and serve him in every way. He was also required to observe the vows of celibacy and poverty and to live by begging for alms. The child learnt humility and became conscious of his indebtedness to society. At the same time society became aware of its responsibilities for the education of the new generation. The *Samavartna* ceremony marked the end of student life and the return home. At this time the student renounced the girdle and took leave of his teacher after offering him *Gurudakshina* according to his means.

From the above it is evident that education was a private affair in which the rulers played no role. They could subsidise educational institutions with grants of land or money but could not impose conditions or control teachers. Teachers and pupils were maintained at public expense and were influenced only by public opinion. The teachers were a highly honoured class; even the kings rose from their thrones to receive them in court. The following verse exemplfies the reverence accorded to them:

> *Gurur Brahma Gurur Vishnu Gurur Devo Mahesvarah*
> *Gurureva Param Brahma Tasmai Sri Gurave Namah*

> (The teacher is Brahma, the teacher is Vishnu, the teacher is the great God Shiva.
> The teacher is the great Brahman-Supreme Divine Soul-incarnate. Bow to that teacher.

The immediate aim of education in ancient India was to prepare children for their roles as members of the castes they were born into and its ultimate aim was *sa vidya ya vimuktye,* meaning knowledge for the emancipation of the soul. The method of study was *shravan, manan, nididhyasan,* i.e., listening to the teacher, reflection on what had been listened to, and its constant repetition. Further, it was not considered enough for a student to merely acquire knowledge; the process of learning was not complete unless the knowledge acquired could be imparted to others.

Girls' education was not as strictly enforced as that of the boys', but they were free to study the Vedas and other subjects along with their brother pupils. The *Artha Veda* says that a girl must not marry until she has completed her studies. It was during the period of Manu that marriage of girls before the age of puberty was sanctioned. Manu held that the marriage of girls was as good as their initiation into the study of the Vedas, serving the husband was as good as education at an Ashram, and performance of household duties as good as religious rituals. The age of patriarchy had begun.

Several hundred years after the Aryans had settled in the Indo-Gangetic plains, and their social system, which was originally grounded on the rational premise of division of labour, had lost its logic, came the invasions of tribes from Central Asia,

Afghanistan, Turkey and the Arabian peninsula. Their religion, Islam, gave the highest status to learning. One of the famous Hadith of Prophet Mohammad was, 'Seek knowledge even if it is in China'. Their system of education was also a private affair. In several other aspects too, parallels may be drawn between Hindu and the Muslim systems of education. Their schools of instruction, Maktabs and Madrasahs were associated with the mosques. There they were taught the Quran, that being regarded in Islam as the fountainhead of all learning. Other subjects like languages, arts and sciences all ensued from the study of the Quran.

In a manner similar to the Hindus, the Muslim child's education began with initiation in religion. The *Bismillah* ceremony was performed at the age of four or five. Whereas the Maktab (the Arabic root word is *kutub*, meaning 'he wrote') was the place where the children learnt the Quran, starting from the Arabic alphabet to the complete *surahs*, the Madrasahs (the Arabic root word is *dars* meaning 'lesson') covered other subjects such as grammar, logic, rhetoric, literature, theology, metaphysics, jurisprudence and medicine. Abul Fazal's *Ain-i-Akbari* gives an account of Akbar's interest in education. The Emperor, though himself unlettered, prescribed the curriculum of studies and included in it subjects of practical value to the student. 'These regulations', writes Abul Fazal, 'shed a new light on schools and cast a bright lustre over Madrasahs'. Since there was no formal arrangement for girls' education they were instructed at home. Examples of princesses like Gulbadan Begum, daughter of Babar, Jahanara, daughter of Shah Jahan and Zebunnisa, daughter of Aurangzeb, testify to the presence of women literati among the aristocracy.

A new era in education began with the arrival of the British. 'Education in India under the British rule', wrote A.P. Howell in *Education in British India*, 'was first ignored, then violently and successfully opposed, then conducted on a system now universally admitted to be erroneous, and finally placed on its present footing'. Its trajectory under the British rule can be divided into four segments, from the early days of the British to 1813, from 1813 to 1853, from 1854 to 1920, and from 1921 to 1947.

During the first period, the East India Company remained indifferent to matters pertaining to education. But when the Company's charter was renewed in 1813, it contained a clause which compelled it to assume responsibility for the education of Indians. During the second period, the provinces were left free to adopt their own educational policies. This resulted in a controversy between those who favoured oriental learning and the use of Sanskrit and Persian and those who favoured the dissemination of Western knowledge through the use of English. The infamous Macaulay's Minute of 1835, deorientalised higher education and encouraged English education for upper classes. 'A single shelf of a good European library', Macaulay wrote, 'is worth the whole native literature of India and Arabia!'

The third period began with Sir Charles Wood's despatch of 1854 and closed with the *Government of India Act 1919*. During this time, the government tried to chalk out and control the educational policy of the country as a whole. Its policy, however, began to be watched very carefully by nationalists for any sign of 'officialised' education. This period is crucial because it coincides with the emergence of Indian nationalism. The agitation over the partition of Bengal in 1905, the emphasis on Swadeshi and boycott of government goods, followed by the Minto-Morley reforms, Non-Cooperation movement and the outbreak of World War I, led to demands for reforming the educational system. Certain fundamental principles of education were clearly stated by the nationalists, such as Indian control, love for the motherland, end of servile imitation, end of domination of English and emphasis on vocational education.

The attempts of educationists and reformers to start national schools fall into two periods. The first active period was soon after the partition of Bengal and the second followed Mahatma Gandhi's preaching of boycott of government schools and colleages, which culminated in the Non-Cooperation resolution passed by Congress in 1920. It earnestly advised the 'gradual withdrawal of children from schools or colleages, owned, aided or controlled by government and in place of such schools and colleges, the establishment of national schools and colleges in the various provinces'. (Pattabhi Sitaramaiyya, *History of Indian National Congress*, Volume 1, page 203.)

It was in the wake of Mahatma Gandhi's appeal that Modern School was born. In the same year certain other institutions were established; National Muslim University of Aligarh (later Jamia Millia Islamia), Gujarat Vidyapith, Bihar Vidyapith, Kashi Vidyapith and other national schools of all grades. They worked independently of the official system, trying to revive the ideals of the ancient Hindu or Muslim education. Schools were established with the Gurukul philosophy of education, Arya Samaj, Sanatan Dharam, Khalsa, and Madrasahs.

In the fourth period, new constitutional reforms envisaged by the Act of 1919, were introduced. It was a period of provincial autonomy when the control and responsibility for education was finally transferred from the Government of India to the provinces. Full provincial autonomy was conceded by the *Government of India Act 1935* whereby large powers were given to the Provincial Ministers of Education. Between 1937 and 1940, when Congress Ministries held office in seven out of eleven provinces, they drew up several schemes for reforming education, including Gandhiji's notion of Basic Education, which became known as the Wardha Scheme. This provided a detailed plan for primary education, based on Gandhian philosophy of learning in the mother tongue and early determination of vocational aptitude. But the Congress Ministries resigned amid political agitation and the Second World War broke out in 1939. The envisaged programme could not be properly implemented. The Government of India, meanwhile, prepared its own plan for educational development. Sir John Sargent, Educational Advisor to the Government of India was asked to prepare a memorandum on 'Post-war educational development in India'. This report, which covered different aspects of the Indian educational problems, became known as the Sargent Report. It wielded a powerful influence on contemporary educational thought.

Several of the schools which today belong to the public school category have evolved from the former Chief's Colleges. Those were institutions of secondary education which were established by the British, following the national uprising of 1857. Their primary purpose was to influence the princely families and gain their political support. They were placed under the supervision of the Political Department of the government. Meant for the education of the sons of princes, sardars, *taluqdars,* and *jagirdars,* they were located in princely states which, after independence, were merged into Rajasthan, Uttar Pradesh, Madhya Pradesh, Andhra Pradesh and Saurashtra. Rajkumar College, the first Chief's College, was founded in 1868 at Rajkot. Mayo College, Ajmer was founded in 1873, Sadul School, Bikaner in 1893, Rajkumar College, Raipur in 1894, Scindia School, Gwalior in 1897, Daly College, Indore in 1898; and two others—Colwin Taluqdars at Lucknow and Jagirdar's at Begumpet—both in 1913. Aitchison Chief's College was established in Lahore. Sons of rulers used to arrive at these educational institutions with armed guards, retinue of servants and private tutors.

Another group of schools were founded to impart a general education and military training to sons of army officers and military personnel. Residential schools, such as Lawrence School Sanawar (1847) and Lawrence School Lovedale (1858) were meant exclusively for Europeans and Anglo-Indians. There was nothing in the public school mould which was accessible to the common people until the appearance of Modern School on the educational scene in 1920. This was ten years prior to the time that witnessed the transfer of Chief's Colleges to modern public schools. This began with a movement initiated in the 1930s by F.C. Pearce of Scindia School, H.W. Barritt of Rajkot, C.H. Barry of Aitchison, Smith-Pearse of Raipur and A.E. Foot of Doon.

In 1921, the year after which Modern School was established, there were, according to the *Quinquennial Review, 1922-27,* 1,55,017 primary schools in the country, and a total enrollment of 61,09,752. This drop-in-the ocean public education at the primary level saw a further decline due to the rise of alternate schools' as stated above. Mahatma Gandhi mobilised the masses by launching his Non-Cooperation Movement. So far as education was concerned, the withdrawal from government and recognised institutions, and repudiation of state grants and recognition were openly advocated. Parallel institutions known as national schools, were set up throughout the country.

It was hoped that these national institutions would breed a new race of Indians with a broad national outlook, free from slavish mentality. Their courses of study did not differ much from the Departmental schools but Hindi was studied as an all-India language instead of English, mother tongue was used as a medium of instruction and the use of *Charkha* was taught as a preliminary step towards economic independence of India from the West. This was the prevailing atmosphere, when Raghubir Singh, who was to found Modern School, wrote these words in his diary:

> We are all aware of the system of education in India. There are four kinds of schools at present; government schools which are entirely financed and managed by the government, schools which require grant-in-aid from government including those run by foreign missions, those maintained by local public bodies, for example, Arya Samaj—independent schools so far as their finances are concerned but controlled in academic matters by the Department or university. The fourth type of schools are those which are conducted by private enterprise and on independent lines, and may be considered experiments in education. Such schools do not follow the common scheme of education but try to chalk out their own lines of work.

It was the last category to which Modern School belonged.

Raghubir Singh was to record the inception of his school in the following words:

> The Modern School was started in 1920 by a body of men who were not satisfied with the existing schools and desired to provide something better for their children.

The Dream Takes Shape

Khushwant Singh

In 1947, appeared a book entitled *A Successful Experiment in Education*. In this book, was a chapter 'Jottings regarding Modern School' on the progress and achievements of Modern School. Among the archives of the Raghubir Singh family, there were other notes written by him from time to time in the year 1917. Together they made up what was essentially Raghubir Singh's philosophy of education. Modern School was in fact started as the model laboratory in which he tested his theories of education.

In 1917, Raghubir Singh undertook an all -India tour to familiarize himself with various educational institutions and places of general historical interest. He put down his impressions on paper, as he went along, revealing a humanistic interest in all that he saw. We gather that he visited the following institutions, Sir Rabindranath Tagore's School at Bolpur, The Cawnpore Theosophical School, Muir Central College, Allahabad, and the Theosophical High School founded by Mrs. Annie Besant at Benaras. He also visited the proposed site of the Benaras Hindu University which he records 'was going to be built on the bank of the Ganges just opposite the Ramnagar Fort'. In Patna he visited the Khuda Bakhsh Library, and recording the thrill of discovering a treasure, wrote :

> I cannot describe the pleasure I felt when I saw some of the manuscripts. I felt as if I could go on looking at them for hours. On account of want of time I had to come away but it is a place where one could spend days without any fatigue.

When he was writing these notes in 1917, he had given serious thought to starting his own school. During his tour he discussed the idea of Modern School (though the name came much later) with Gurudev Rabindranath Tagore, who encouraged the young man to go ahead. Based on what he found in the schools he visited, he felt that there was need for a school in which the modern view of education would blend with the goodness of the Indian traditional approach. The diary referred to above, is dated 9 November 1919, and the notes written in it were meant to be given to his father. Sultan Singh was partly responsible for planting the idea in his mind and it was his guidance and approval that Raghubir valued beyond anything else in his life. We have no evidence whether or not the notes reached his father but the fact is that Sultan Singh graciously agreed to meet all the requirements which would enable his son to start the institution.

The second important factor, which led to the establishment of Modern School, was Raghubir Singh's own intense involvement in bringing up his three children for whom he took on the role of both parents because of the continuing indisposition of his wife. In his mind he had evolved for them a system of education taking into account the shortcomings of traditional approaches to education and the need to retain some of the western ideas on the subject. From his random notes written in two periods, 1917 and 1919, it has been possible to reconstruct his concept of education, to which he strove to give concrete shape in Modern School.

'A sound system of National Education', he wrote, 'is the foundation upon which the fabric of any progressive state exists and unless the government or the people are able to organise the educational system, progress is not possible... . The origin of present educational system, is to produce clerks. It is not real education. It was made possible by our slave mentality, a natural corollory of foreign rule and later on because of sheer economic necessity'. He asked what is real education? Is it knowledge for its own sake or for gaining money? 'We have lost sight of real education because our immediate objective is to pass examinations and our ultimate aim is government appointment.' He says that there is nothing more debilitating for the student than cramming texts. Under a system in which the curriculum is entirely bookish many able boys may lose all interest in their work. He deplores that the shadow of the examination is rarely lifted and considerable time of the teachers and students is spent in imparting or receiving private tuition. 'It is the dread of these examinations that clouds the horizon of (Indian) boys during their whole school career. What should be the happiest period of life (and is so in other countries where more fortunate conditions prevail) becomes a life of drudgery and overstrain.' The parents and guardians have accepted this system of education as a *fait accompli* and do not demand a change. 'On account of an evil tradition we have to guard against the mania of examinations which prevails so much in the country and remember that in real life it is personal merit and not so much the possession of a certificate that counts.'

He deplores the fact that school education is not supplemented by sending children to tramp in the hills or by encouraging them to follow hobbies in their spare time. They never care to go out even when there is a chance of gain nor do they have the curiousity for sight-seeing or travelling. By the time a young man has completed his education, Raghubir Singh wrote, he is a product turned out by a lifeless machine, exactly like so many others. The other burden is that of marriage which is thrust upon him too early, clipping his wings precisely when he ought to have felt free like a bird.

When the state of education is so deficient, he asks, how can the youth be expected to mount a struggle for freedom against a foreign power? 'A country where its youth are crushed under a deadly system and all spirit of adventure crushed out of them....cannot hope to rise from slavery and fight against the most daring, stubborn and adventurous nation in the world.'

The admission policy which was followed in Modern School owed its origin to Raghubir Singh's belief that the education of a child begins from the moment it is born. He wrote at length about the upbringing of the child from its infancy and the role particularly of the mother. 'Up to the age of five or six the child remains at home and the responsibility of its training devolves on the parents. The greatest amount of attention is required at this stage and any trouble taken is sure to amply repay the parents in providing character for the little ones and comfort and leisure for the parents.' But the training at this stage, he felt, was the one most neglected; and an unstable foundation was, therefore, laid. He wrote that due to the indifference of the parents, children are allowed to grow like 'wild plants' and in some cases they have to be saved from the 'evil influence of their own homes'. To avoid this he envisaged a nursery school for children aged three to seven years.

Lack of educational facilities for women, he wrote, placed them at a disadvantage in their marriage in which they were not able to become real friends, mutual helpers, often making unhappy homes. Women were oppressed and treated as objects for the satisfaction of men's fancies. They were kept in darkness about the world and always suppressed their feelings, resulting in a lack of harmony in the home and absence of happiness. This incompatibility had a natural debilitating effect on the children.

On the question of discipline, he believes that the child should be helped to evolve a discipline of the mind which would enable him to distinguish between 'The beautiful and the ugly, the tidy and the chaotic'. That is preferable to imposing external discipline. We cannot mould the child into the pattern we desire, he wrote, we have to allow him to grow along his own bent. 'You should not run contrary to his grain, as by doing so you arouse contrary forces and you hinder rather than help the growth.' The two essential factors of discipline are to think hard before imposing our will and to be firm in carrying out the punishment that the breach of discipline entails. Another factor is that the child should recognize our rules and commands to be reasonable. Unless that is achieved, the punishment would have an adverse effect. In the matter of discipline and punishment the help of his fellows and team mates may be taken because of the child's desire for approval of his peers.

Certain ideals of Raghubir Singh formed the bedrock of the proposed school. First, education was to be imparted on the most liberal lines and all those engaged in the task of carrying on the institution were to be free from the prejudice of caste, colour race or country. Commenting on the adverse use of religion, he writes:

> Religion has always excited the greatest sentiments and often leads people to

> a kind of prejudice, resulting in an undue bias for a particular doctrine which they profess to believe and a hatred towards those who do not follow their creed. In India, people are particularly prone to drift into religious controversies and it is suggested that the doctrines of no particular religion be taught in the school; the moral development being trusted to the general atmosphere of the place.

Then he makes an important statement about the identical essence of all religious faiths :

> It is not so much the reading of any book or the outward following of a ceremonial, that makes a man religious but it is the spirit with which he goes about in the world and does even the common duties of everyday life that raises or degrades him, and this is the essence of all religions.

Respect for an enlightened faith rather than ritualistic conformity, which is the hallmark of today's Modern School, is the legacy of Raghubir Singh's concept of religion. It is marked by a rejection of blind faith which contravenes rational and enlightened thinking. During his 1917 tour, he wrote:

> Devotion, generally blind, towards their gods, or any other substitute for such a Being—this leads into a spirit of religion commonly met with all over India and the desire to follow all that is old, leading people to stick to innumerable ceremonies (which are mostly absurd) simply because they are put down in some book which they regard as sacred. 'Anything that is old must be good'.

Secondly he dwells upon, the selection of teachers.

> The success of a school entirely depends upon the capacities and personalities of the teachers and great care will have to be exercised in their proper selection.

He wants to see men and women of character appointed, who have made teaching the ideal of their lives. The two qualities they must engender in their students, are character and morality. He believes that the high moral tone of the school must be maintained and the teacher can do it with love and sympathy. To explain the student-teacher relationship, he uses the analogy of a gardener tending his plants. His advice to the teachers is basically two-fold. First, to be 'punctilious and exact' in their own work so that they can infuse the same in the students. Second, not to allow their personal setbacks to intrude upon their dealings with the pupils. He considers sympathy to be the 'greatest quality one human being can show to another' and recommends it as the bonding factor between the student and the teacher.

The school, he says, should have a liberal mandate and provide scope for educational experimentation. He refers again and again to freedom to advance in the direction of truth and knowledge, which reflects his desire that the school should break free from the fetters of over-regulation. 'It should be free from the fetters of official or public control so that in time it could work out its own destiny.'

Coming to the specifics, he places equal emphasis on training in the mother tongue as well as English. Among the academic subjects he mentions all but emphasizes science, and states that the student should be encouraged to gain detailed knowledge of the branch of science that he is most interested in. He is keen that there be training in fine arts, in anatomy and physiology, first aid and nursing; equally important is introduction to the 'science of sex'.

Extra-curricular activities are considered important for overall development. Physical development is particularly important because the 'Indian child is physically very weak. Scouting expeditions, trips for nature study or to places of historical interest are considered of great educational value. Dramatics is a useful tool of instruction and the 'cinematograph' should be used for teaching as well. The school should provoke the student to discover his special aptitude, 'what he should become in life for which he could prepare himself further, and enter life with a firm resolve to make a success of the vocation he has chosen.'

The ideal location of the school would be a hill station, he wrote, but Delhi has certain advantages, so the school may be started here. During the hot weather he suggests, that the school be moved to a cool climate after one month of summer vacation and 'reopen at headquarters during the month of October'. Elaborating on the advantage of this routine he wrote:

> Opportunities for an outdoor life and Nature Study will be ample. A rambling trip in the mountains or a visit to some snow peak will do a lot of good to the health of the boys and give them opportunities of an adventurous and manly life.

The natural corollary to this scheme was that the school should essentially be residential except in very rare cases when some students may be admitted as day scholars. The tuition fees were to be Rs. 20 and the hostel fees Rs. 40. The Principal would work in an honorary capacity. The most qualified teacher would draw a salary of Rs. 200. Total cost of equipment needed in the first five years was estimated at Rs. 6000. The salaries of academic and non-academic staff were totalled at Rs. 1500. Starting with an enrolment of ten to fifteen students in the first year, the total strength at the end of five years was estimated at sixty. With a capital investment of Rs. 25,000 to 30,000 the school was expected to run for five years after which it would become self supporting.

The specific request by the son to his father was two-fold. First, to permit the use of their Daryaganj house at a reasonable rent. Second to invest the required amount himself or obtain it from friends without allowing them undue interference in the management.

The School Begins

Rev. C.F. Andrews

More than thirty years ago Rai Bahadur Lala Sultan Singh was in London with Principal Sushil Kumar Rudra and myself. He asked me if it would be possible to find someone who could undertake tutorial work with his son Raghubir and also help him in the college. My friend Willie Pearson had been sent home ill with rheumatism and lumbago from Bhowanipore, Calcutta. His health was still far from good, but it seemed to all of us that the light tutorial work in a dry and sunny climate, during the cold weather at Delhi, might be more invigorating for him than any immediate return to Calcutta. The experiment was tried and was quite successful. The cold weather in Delhi and the hot weather in Kashmir restored Willie to perfect health. It seemed to me also, as I watched his recovery, that the joy of being able to return to India was the best medicine of all. He seemed to get well from the first day that we started back for the East.

This incident in London marked the beginning of a deep friendship between tutor and pupil. Raghubir was too young in 1913 to realize all that it meant to have Willie Pearson as a friend and a tutor, during that one short year from November 1912 to November 1913. But at a later time (after the War) in England, in 1922, he came again under the spell of Willie's magnetic personality. Thoughts that were beginning to shape themselves in his mind then came to their birth.

Thus Bengal gave Willie Pearson to Delhi for a short season, and out of that visit many important events happened. One of these was the fact that in November 1913, Willie Pearson was set free from his tutorial work and was able to accompany me to South Africa. But the event about which I am writing in this present article was quite different. It was this. He had a unique influence on Raghubir at the most impressionable time of his life. He did not check but on the other hand actively encouraged the boy's ideas of serving humanity. Thus, when he grew up, the needs of his country awakened in him the love of service. He became unwilling to throw all his time into the banking profession, which each generation of his family had followed hitherto. He sought a wider outlet for public service.

His father, Sultan Singh, had an idealist side to his nature; and this was shared also by Raghubir's mother, who was at one with her husband in his wider purposes at the time when he broke through many old restrictions. Thus it became easier for Raghubir himself to break through the orthodox barriers when the opportunity came. His grandmother remained strictly orthodox throughout her long life and her religious duties were her one great consolation in her old age. Her son and grandson held her in deep reverence and she passed away in peace.

How great a wrench it was to her when the younger generations of her family departed from orthodoxy, few are able to realize today. For such acts have become far more common and less noticeable than they were in those earlier days. But the step having once been taken, there was no turning back.

At the same time, neither Raghubir nor his father were among those who changed everything they had, such as food, dress, language, for the sake of being regarded as 'up-to-date' and 'modern' in the wrong sense of the word. In all essential respects they remained Indian both in manners and customs. The conservative element which was always very strong in their family kept the balance and prevented the pendulum from swinging too far in the direction of change. In every essential respect they remained true to their own country's history and requirements.

Raghubir, in his revolt from orthodoxy, had determined that his own children should be brought up from the very first in a modern atmosphere without the trammels which had hindered his own earliest progress. His own father was still living. With his parents' cordial consent and co-operation he determined to start the Modern School. From its foundation onwards he has had the support of Miss K. Bose, who has been the head mistress of the school, and has given her whole life to its successful development. Without her personality and genius the work could never have been carried forward to its present remarkable stage of rapid progress.

The Modern School was founded in 1920. Its first home was at Daryaganj, Delhi, not far from the house of Dr. Ansari. It aimed at creating a new type of education at the centre of Indian administration. The idea of education which it embodied might almost be summed up in the words so often quoted from the New Testament. 'I am come that they may have life and I have it more abundantly'. From the very first the school was to be open to children of all religious denominations. It was to be entirely unsectarian in character. Hindus, Muslims, Parsees, Christians—all were welcome.

It has been a great joy to me from the very first to see in this school the religious barriers entirely broken down among the children who are taught to respect and understand the faiths of other people. There is no attempt whatsoever to proselytise. At the same time there is a distinct religious atmosphere, with simple daily prayers addressed to the One Father of all mankind. During all these years, the religious difficulty has never been apparent. The children grow up without a trace of the old narrowness that used to keep them so much apart.

The Modern School was founded in this manner. Certain wealthy citizens of

Delhi had approached Lala Sultan Singh with regard to the formation of a Modern School for their children. Raghubir undertook to create the school if support was offered in full measure. On the whole the City of Delhi has given its strong approval to the new venture.

In the earliest days the school buildings were hardly sufficient to contain the children. But in 1933 a glorious opportunity of expansion arose and a new site was provided in Barakhamba Road, New Delhi, covering twenty-five acres of land for a completely new school with playing grounds and hostels attached. Ten acres has already been set apart for school sports and a great portion of the buildings has already been created. The school is quite close to the quarters where the permanent government officials of New Delhi are in residence and many of their children already attend the school. But the greater proportion come from Older Delhi and the citizens of the ancient city give the school enthusiatic support.

One of the parents has already promised to build a gymnasium and other parents have made similar offers. The teachers have the interest of the school at heart and are all devoted to their work. The ideal represented in the school is similar to that known as the *Ecole Nouvelle* on the continent of Europe, and the New Education Fellowship in England. By far the larger proportion of the children are infants because the whole principle of education represented depends upon early training. Unless the creative habit of thought and action is produced in the children at a very early age, they cannot gain the benefit of freedom which the New Education System offers. The whole method is made to depend upon this freedom.

When I visited the school quite recently, what struck me immediately was the happiness of the children whom I met, especially the youngest infants. They flocked around me at once without any shyness at all and held up their hands with the little toys and clay models which they had made. These were wonderfully constructed and it was a great delight to see such complete happiness in their faces. They were evidently proud of their own master-work and the joy of showing these models had turned the school-work into a glorious game. It was clear to me that they would not miss their school lessons for anything else in the world.

The greatest care is taken with the youngest children. It is realized that they need far more continuous attention than the older boys and girls. With their abundant energy they occupy every moment of the teacher's time and their eagerness to accomplish the tasks which they are given to do is apparent. Some of these infants are brought each day to the school in the lorry which collects them each morning and takes them back each evening. Others who are older come on bicycles. In addition, a large number of children are boarders. When all the buildings are finished, it is proposed to have a series of hostels for boys and girls. The school is co-educational throughout.

It is impossible in one article to explain the methods of study and the care that is taken of the physical fitness of the children. Nothing is done to make the life of the child either comfort-loving or lacking in hard discipline. At the same time the children are encouraged to get all the fun out of life, which it is possible to obtain. Those who would wish to learn more, should write to the school secretary at Barakhamba Road, New Delhi. It is impossible to congratulate too highly Miss K. Bose and Lala Raghubir Singh on their splendid achievement. It is my great hope that they both may be able, by years of self-sacrificing work, to see the school firmly established. No greater benefit than this could come to the citizens of Old Delhi who have to face with their families the modern conditions of life.

*The Modern School: An Interesting Educational Experiment**

The Speech Day of the Modern School came off this afternoon. The School Committee were At Home, to a very large and representative gathering of guests, both European and Indian ladies and gentlemen. Among those present were Sir Muhammad Shafi, Kanwar and Kanwarani Maharaj Singh, Dr. Besant, many members of the Legislative Assembly and the Council of State. Some very well rendered displays in drill, Montessori methods, art work and music were given by the pupils. Perhaps the most appreciated was the excellent performances given by the little ones in instrumental music, which with painting is compulsory for each pupil.

Sir Muhammad Shafi made a brief speech before the conclusion of the function, congratulating the managing committee and the staff of the school, on the great and rapid success of their undertaking, which he considered was a most patriotic venture.

This institution, almost the only one of its kind in North India, constitutes a most interesting experiment, and has great possiblilities in the educational future of the country. It was started in October 1920, independent of any existing organisation but with a first rate staff and the most up to date equipment and fittings. No outside help was asked for, the promoters and the parents of the pupils bearing the entire cost of putting the school on its feet. It started with twelve children, sons or daughters of the local gentry; the number has by now risen to thirty-five, ten of them being little girls and two are Europeans. There is still room for another twenty-five or thirty children who as a rule are not admitted after the age of eight. There are four resident pupils who come from outside Delhi and the school offers home care and comforts to children sent from other stations.

Freedom of Text Books

The teachers are given complete freedom to choose their own text books and to follow the methods of instruction they think best in their subjects, sufficient latitude being allowed in the time table. One of the strongest sides of the school work is the Montessori Class for which a fully qualified Montessori mistress, was brought out

---

* This article appeared in *The Civil and Military Gazette,* Tuesday, February 20, 1923

from England last year. The school is bilingual from the very beginning, the children being taught to speak English and Hindi very naturally and with great ease. Vocal music is compulsory and the older children receive instruction in instrumental music. A small school orchestra will be organised in the near future. Considering the fact that all the scholars come from rich homes, where they as a rule do hardly anything with their own hands, the school authorities have been very wise in setting apart one hour every day for manual work in which every child has to take part according to his age. Boys above eight years of age have to work in the carpentry workshop three times a week and at gardening the other three days. Referring to the health of the pupils the Secretary made a striking statement in the course of his report. He said, 'The beneficial effect of the school on the health of the children is demonstrated from the fact, that whenever there have been any long holidays the weight curve on the charts, in most cases, has shown a tendency to go down. It has invariably risen again after the school has reopened. The regular life in the school has a decided effect for the better'.

The school staff consist of a qualified lady Principal, two qualified lady teachers and four masters. The tuition fees for each pupil have so far been Rs. 50 per mensem which also includes the cost of meals supplied during school hours. In order to enlarge the scope of the school, the committee has reduced fees for new admissions from Rs. 50 to Rs. 35.

The school, supplying as it does a long-felt want for a first rate preparatory school for the children of Indian gentry, needs to be given every encouragement. It does not ask for any Government aid at present as it is felt that the requirements of the Education Code are too rigid for the development of a novel experiment of this kind. The Superintendent of Education, Delhi, in the course of his last quinquennial report spoke of this institution as an experiment which constitutes constructive criticism of the present system.

The First Years

Raghubir Singh

In order to explain just when and how the idea of starting a school such as this, came into my mind, it will be necessary for me to hark back to my own student days and to recall what I owe to the inspiration of my old teachers and friends, the late Principal S.K. Rudra, C.H.C. Sharp and the late Mr. W.W. Pearson. To the last named, whom I was so fortunate as to have as my tutor when I was at college, I owe more than I fully know or realise for implanting in my mind educational ideas which I have never ceased to cherish. At first, no doubt, unconsciously rather than consciously, but not for long. Finding myself faced, before many years had passed, with the problem of determining upon what lines the education of my own little ones should be planned, a problem which had hitherto been theoretical and academic, at once assumed for me a very practical shape.

My immediate concern being more especially with infant education, it was the Montessori system that first engaged my attention. I studied much of the literature on the subject, and for the benefit of my own little children, was at pains to see that their classroom was furnished with all the requisite equipment, material and apparatus. But it was impossible for me to rest satisfied with that. The need for a well-conceived scheme of education having been brought home to me in my own personal experience as a parent, it was impossible for me not to desire that the advantage of an education which had proved so full of promise for my children, should be extended to as large a circle as possible.

It was now that I become aware of an urge, growing even more insistent, to devote my life to educational work. After making myself thoroughly conversant with various aspects of educational problems, I was able to arrive at certain definite conclusions of my own; while the warm encouragement that I received from a highly respected school teacher of my own boyhood, gave me added confidence in addressing myself to so arduous an undertaking as that of endeavouring to realise in concrete reality the ideal school of my dreams.

For some type of school education, conceived on large and liberal lines, the need was indeed already sufficiently apparent. It had long been felt by many thoughtful persons that if the Indians were to discharge their civic responsibilities created by the changing political conditions, in both the civil and military spheres of national life, the younger generation must be provided with a better system of education, where the physical, mental and spiritual faculties might have the fullest scope for development. Under existing circumstances, such a liberal education was hardly obtainable. The difficulty of finding a really first class school with modern equipment, and teachers qualified on all sides for their task, had long been felt by parents who were keen on a sound education for their children, especially those of a tender age. It was this common difficulty which brought together a few parents in the endeavour to solve a common problem; and it was in their joint effort at a solution that the Modern School had its inception.

Inspired with such aims and ideals and urged on with a keen sense of the need of an improved type of education not only for their own children but for all children destined to be, in any sense, leaders in the India of tomorrow, the founders of the school and the promoters of the scheme made a start.

The first step was to appoint a Principal, and here the Society was fortunate in securing the services of Miss Kamala Bose, who ever since her appointment in this capacity, has been working with indefatigable devotion for the well-being and development of the school.

With an eye primarily to the education of their own children, this group of parents were led, after due deliberation, to start a new type of school independent of any existing organisation. But once started, the school was bound to throw open its doors to the public without distinction of caste, colour or creed, and was so organised as to enable the child to learn through life itself, and to live abundantly, and thereby to gain a sense of the wholeness of life. For a school, professing such an aim, no location could be imagined more suitable than Delhi so rich in historical associations, and yet—as the hub of the country's political life, and a notable centre of its intellectual activity—so progressive in its outlook. As embodying in its own sphere a 'forward looking mind,' the school may claim, we hope, to be not unworthy of the name bestowed upon it, by those to whom it owed its foundation, 'The Modern School'.

Thus it was that the school came into existence. In August 1920, the Modern School Society was registered under Act XXI of 1860 and the school actually commenced work from the 20th October 1920 with an infant class of about six children on the rolls (the number swelled up to twelve by the end of the year)—all of them children of persons specially interested in the scheme, in one of the old 19th century bungalows which was in the south-east angle of the city wall and belonged to our family. These children besides receiving instruction in the ordinary subjects of the Primary School education were also taught elementary forms of kindergarten handicrafts. They had certain periods allotted for play. This infant class came to school at 8 a.m. and remained till about 6 in the evening. They had one meal all together at mid-day and refreshments in the afternoon.

It was the intention of the promoters of the school to run it for at least three years as an experimental measure; and if the result proved satisfactory, to put it on to a permanent basis by housing it in a building of its own and by building up an adequate endowment. No outside help was asked for at the outset, the idea being to organise the school and realise in the actual working the ideals aimed at, before issuing any appeal for funds.

For nearly thirteen years, this bungalow, 24 Daryaganj, was the home of the Modern School. From the small beginnings of 1920 it had already developed by 1932 into a good-sized school. In 1932, the number of scholars on the rolls was about one hundred and twenty-five.

The persons interested in starting the school had full confidence in me, and allowed me to carry out my ideas and organise the school according to my plans. My idea was to get small children and train them from their very infancy. I also decided to start from the lower classes only and to add one class each year as the school progressed, and to let it develop eventually into a high school, to which the two Intermediate classes could finally be attached.

A syllabus of subjects to be taught was drawn up for the school by the Education Sub-Committee composed of the late R.S. Ratan Lal, Mr. C.H.C. Sharp, Rai Bahadur N.K. Sen, Miss K. Bose, Pandit Har Narain Shastri, Maulvi Abdul Rahman and myself.

At the very beginning of the school's existence, it was decided that it should be a Day Boarding School. The intention was to make sure that the children should enjoy to the full the benefits which it was the purpose of the school to impart; that for as many hours of the day as possible they should be living in the healthy physical, mental and moral environment of the school precincts, but without losing touch with their homes.

The school was to be not just a place where they were to learn their lessons, but a place where they should also rest, play, have their meals together and enjoy the manifold benefits of happy association with their fellows in all the interests of their common life. It was in fact to be to them a second home. Coming to school early in the morning at 8, they would return home about 6 in the evening. And yet while the school should be essentially a Day Boarding School, some provision, it was felt, should be made for full time boarders.

Children from all over India have been admitted to the school from time to time, and at present most provinces of India and all communities (Hindus, Muslims, Jains, Sikhs, Parsis, Christians etc.) are represented amongst the children. It is desired that the atmosphere of the home should prevail in the school, and it is thought that the wholesome influence of the boys and girls on each other would help in creating an all-round individual, who would have a natural and healthy outlook on life. Hence both boys and girls are admitted.

For pupils coming from outside Delhi, arrangements are made to keep them in the school hostel. Every child in the main school has to be a day boarder, they come in the morning after a light breakfast and go home in the evening after games in time for dinner. It is not compulsory for children in the Primary School to stay for the whole day. It is desired to place the children in a progressive environment, where development of character is valued more than formal instruction.

On the lines above indicated, the school has functioned for the greater part of its existence. But while the hostel still functions and flourishes, exigencies of war-time economy (rationing, etc.) have necessitated the temporary and partial discontinuance of common meals for the whole school. This modification of the original whole-day school time-table is purely temporary. As soon as possible, the school may revert to the old system. The present multilated time-table is interim and provisional.

But while certain features of the school life have suffered (inevitably) some temporary curtailment, the basic aims and ideals of the school remain unaltered. The whole educational effort continues to be animated with the aims and ideals of earlier years. These have already been comprehensively, if not concisely, defined as follows:

> The school is based upon ideals of education wider than those which can be embodied in any formal curriculum of instruction, and attempts to carry them out by free and more diversified methods than can be found in most existing schools. It aims at giving a continuous education to its scholars from infancy to the conclusion of the school age. In the lowest stages, the school is conducted on the Montessori and Froebel systems.
>
> It is desired that a child may have full scope for development—physical, mental, moral and spiritual—in an atmosphere of freedom, where it has opportunities for self-expression, and is above everything else happy. Throughout, the main object of teaching is to make the students interested in the subjects taught, which in itself ensures progress, as a child who takes delight in its work can assimilate knowledge more easily than one who is working under compulsion.
>
> Children are encouraged to do their own work and the bigger boys are appointed to supervise various duties in the school and the Boarding House. Sometimes they clean the rooms to get accustomed to doing things with their own hands. The boys are being trained to be self-reliant, so that as they grow up they could be entrusted with greater responsibility.

It is in accordance with these ideals of freedom and diversity that the school, while it has drawn freely upon its own experience, has also imbibed systems and methods that have been successfully developed in western countries. There has been a conscious attempt to follow the newer and more modern methods of education, especially in individual attention to each pupil and allowing as much free play as possible to the natural bent of each. In a word the basis of the system is similar to that known as the *Ecole Nouvelle* on the continent, the system represented by the New Education Fellowship in England or progressive education in the United States.

From this it follows that the Modern School is in no sense a public school. Setting a high value on home influences, and paying individual attention to the particular requirements of individual pupils, whom it declines to coerce with procrustean rigour into conformity with a standardised system, admirable in many ways but lacking in elasticity, the Modern School parts company with the common run of Public School, while pursuing with no less singleness of purpose its aim of turning little children into good citizens and honourable gentlemen.

*A Plea For Educational Reform In India**

Kamala Bose

The urgent need of India today is not *more* of education, but also of *better* education. The improvement of educational methods must keep pace with the extension of its domain if the best results are to be obtained. This aspect of the problem should be recognised without further delay. In fact, it has been too long delayed already, and the country is suffering from its ill-effects. If the education imparted to the people has been seriously lacking in quantity, it has been still more sadly wanting in quality. This fact impresses one more and more as one gets a closer acquaintance with our educational system. It is specially true about the early stages of education from the primary to the high school standard. The sooner the remedy is found, the better will grow the prospect before the nation.

I have been in educational work in different parts of the country during the last fifteen years, and my experience extends to such diverse places as Calcutta, Eastern Bengal, United Provinces and the Punjab. I have been in charge of the Modern High School at Delhi, which is conducted on new methods, since its inception seven years ago. I have taken part in the education of boys, girls and *purdanashin* women through their school and college courses. So I have had ample occasions for studying and observing the methods and results of our educational system at close quarters, and may fairly claim to have an intimate knowledge of our educational problems. I have also recently had a unique opportunity of studying the educational systems in vogue in Europe, and of seeing the improvements which have been brought about in different places by changes in the school methods. After attending the World Conference on New Education which was held at Locarno in August last, I was able to visit quite a number of schools in Italy, Switzerland, Germany, Holland, Belgium, England and Scotland, including some of the most up-to-date and improved types. It was, therefore, possible to compare the newer methods with the older ones, and to find out the difference in the results obtained. These visits have helped me also to compare the educational methods followed in India with those in Europe, and to realise more vividly the deficiences under which

* This article appeared in *The Modern Review*, February, 1928

we labour here.

The most prominent fact which stands out from a comparison between the progress of education in India and Europe is the utter illiteracy of the masses here. It hangs as a millstone on the neck of India's progress, and must be removed as soon as practicable. As the distances of time and space disappear with improvements in the means of communication, the economic competition between the peoples of the world grows keener every day. India has to enter this area with a serious handicap. She bears a solid block of three hundred million people, i.e., over ninety per cent of her population in a state of absolute ignorance. They do not even possess the rudiments of knowledge, and are, therefore, bereft of any means of self-improvement. Her place in the struggle is almost a hopeless one. Unless a radical and rapid change is brought about, there is great danger that her people will be left far behind in the race. Already the lowliest forms of manual work with the scantiest remuneration fall to the average lot of her industrious workmen. The people might in the end become a nation of hewers of wood and drawers of water—held in the grip of an economic slavery under the advanced nations of the world. In fact, outside India they are already regarded as such by the capitalists in the different parts of the Empire. And with the rapid industrialisation of India by foreign capitalists, the process is going apace within the borders of India herself. Thus the illiteracy of India has proved a real menace unto herself. The situation is a tragic one, but its intensity is further heightened by the fact that in spite of their illiteracy, the intellectual capacity of the masses is of a high order. Even the peasants and the backward classes have given repeated proofs that they are capable of receiving the highest education that can be given them, and of showing splendid results. The same can also be said about the women, who have, with very few exceptions, been almost entirely left in the darkness of ignorance. The University results have shown that their intellectual powers, when given proper scope, are in no way inferior to those of the men.

Universal primary education is the one thing needful for the uplift in India. In order to ensure its rapid progress, it should be made both free and compulsory at first. As a serious matter which concerns the continuance of the Indian people within the civilised circle of the world, the cost of such education should be made the first charge on the revenues of the country. But this education must be something quite different from what is imparted at present. Education, to be effective, must help in creating an alertness of all the senses. This can only come through a very careful development of both the body and the mind of the child. Under our present system in India, a child of tender age is daily confined in a badly constructed and ill-ventilated *pathshala* for long hours without any arrangement for tiffin. He is cramped into a little space and made to acquire a smattering of the Three R's under the shadow of the teacher's birch. He finds no real interest or pleasure in his studies, and simply goes through them as a result of cruel intimidation, which almost shatters his nerves and dampens his lively juvenile spirit. There is hardly any effort made to draw out and develop the natural intelligence of the child. No scope is given him for self-expression. Most of his lessons he has to learn by rote, and has to repeat them to his teacher in a state of nervous fear. No attempt is made to encourage or develop his aesthetic ideas. The curriculum takes no notice of that side of his life. His moral and religious training is left out altogether. Little or no encouragement is given to sports, as being detrimental to study. Physical culture receives no attention. A training in practical co-operation among the boys is never attempted. No real *ésprit de corps* is created. Instead of teaching the dignity of labour, a spirit of contempt for manual work is often fostered. Weak in body and depressed in mind, the child passes through the different stages of his school life, without finding in them much difference as regards method or scope. The higher grade schools are as backward in all these essential matters as the primary ones. On the other hand, as the medium of instruction is changed from the vernacular to a foreign language, the difficulties are further accentuated. When at last the boy comes out of the high school grindmill, there is little of initiative or zest for work left in him. It is no wonder that the Indians have been charged with a lack of originality and initiative. These faults, if true, must be laid at the door of their system of education, which is eminently suited to crush out such qualities. The result of such education has been far from helpful in really building up the nation and has even proved a hindrance in some respects. A good percentage of the primary scholars, finding no incentive to self-culture, gradually forget their lessons, and drift back into illiteracy. The trouble taken to educate them means so much labour lost and money wasted. Others who are able to continue their studies in high schools come out of them merely crammed with some book knowledge, fitted to become petty clerks in offices and shops. They often find their life a failure because their education has not been a preparation for life as all true education should be. While their memories have been sharpened, no serious endeavour has been made to develop the creative faculties of their mind. Such students, even when they get into the college cannot fully recover their powers, which are stunted during their childhood, the most sensitive period of their life. Thus the miserable apology for a school which has been put up in this country, in contrast to the well-planned and fully equipped institution as one finds it in England and elsewhere has retarded the vigorous mental growth of the people. The deficiencies of our system become at once manifest to us as one visits the splendid schools of the West, specially the modern ones, and comes across the healthy, alert and active students there.

If we desire to see our people reach a status equal to that attained by the people of Western countries, we should reform our schools on modern improved lines. In order to do so the following considerations should be specially kept in view:-

(1) A school, in order to be an efficient nursery for the physical and mental

growth of its pupils, must be located on ample grounds. The study of dead records called books, unless accompanied by a simultaneous study of Nature around us, fails to sharpen the faculties of the mind. It leads to a tendency for cramming without a real understanding of the contents. The school grounds, when thoughtfully laid out, provide the children with a suitable field for such nature study. These also create a sense of freedom in the child mind which cannot be found in mere school-rooms. The growing self-consciousness of the child finds scope for development in a little world of its own. Here Nature supplements the education of the child with many valuable lessons which cannot be provided by any human agency, and which bring real joy to the youthful heart. The sceneries, the birds and small animals, the plants and trees, the leaves and flowers, the music provided by some rivulet or the songs of birds—all these make valuable contributions to the intellectual and emotional culture of the child. The child is led gradually to modes of self-expression through arts, such as music and painting. An interest in creative activities is fostered through gardening, etc.

Besides, extensive school grounds are absolutely necessary for maintaining the health and developing the physique of the children. Open air life and outdoor games are essential if a healthy mind is to be preserved in a healthy body. It is only the open fields which can give birth to the spirit of 'sportsmanship'—a term which includes many moral qualities. In Italy, Germany, England and other countries of Europe the utility of extensive school grounds has been fully realised. All good modern schools have large areas of land attached to them. I have there come across schools with less than a hundred pupils which possess a hundred to two hundred acres of land. Much emphasis is placed on this matter, and it is held that the first heavy outlay on it is fully repaid by the improvement in the health and the proper mental growth of a succession of students.

In India there is as much need for school grounds as in Europe, specially in the towns and cities. In rural areas, however, where natural sceneries abound, a smaller quantity of land will generally suffice.

(2) The study of Nature should be further encouraged by means of well arranged excursions to places of natural or historical interest. Such outings form a regular feature of school life in Europe. These are very helpful in quickening the minds of the pupils. Visits to the seaside, hills and lakes, etc., prove useful for the study of elementary geology and geography, while a vivid interest in history is created by seeing places of historical importance. The benefit to the health of the students is also seen in a greater activity and buoyancy among them.

(3) The knowledge of a still wider world should be conveyed to the children through carefully selected magic lantern and cinema exhibitions. These tend to expand their minds very quickly, and enable them to realise the facts regarding other lands more easily than through the medium of books. In Europe such means

are widely adopted for the spread of mass education, and for developing the minds of children. The importance of such methods has hardly yet been realised in this country. Here we have a potent instrument for the rapid extension of education among the masses.

(4) A school should pay proper attention to the health and physique of the pupils. They should undergo medical examination at regular intervals, and be treated for their defects and diseases. The physical exercise of the students should be considered a subject of prime importance in every school, and not a matter of indifference as at present. This should be a regular part of the school curriculum. Gymnastics, athletics, sports, swimming, boating and other healthy games, both indoor and outdoor, should be encouraged. The spirit of sportsmanship should be carefully developed. Due care should also be taken that the food given to the children be suitable and sufficient. It would be desirable to make provision for tiffin for all pupils. It is idle to expect proper mental work on an empty stomach. A school should at least supply free tiffin to all poor students who cannot afford it.

(5) The spirit of co-operation and social service should be inculcated among the pupils from their early childhood. It is wonderful to see how quickly they pick up this training and genuinely fall in with such ideas. Once learnt, the spirit grows with the life of the students, and permeates the whole school. It engenders toleration, and creates a bond of fellowship among them. The school life affords many opportunities for undertaking co-operative and social work among the students themselves.

(6) The students should, apart from their studies, daily engage in some creative activities, viz., gardening, carpentry, smithy, printing, drawing, painting, pottery, photography, weaving, etc. Such work develops the powers of initiative and thought. It also reveals the direction in which the taste of a pupil lies. The scope for manual work which it gives is a healthy corrective against a sedentary education. It further establishes the connection of education with the practical side of life, and makes education more complete than it would otherwise be.

(7) Every effort should be made to develop the aesthetic sense of the pupil, which often lies dormant in him. The realisation of a sense of the beautiful, whether in music, painting, or natural scenery, is essential, and should always be kept in view. Subjects which encourage this process should form a regular part of the curriculum. Thus only can the full mental growth of a child be assured.

(8) As much of the early education as possible should be imparted through object lessons. This will not only make it more interesting, but will keep it from growing purely abstract and from encouraging cramming.

(9) To obtain the best results it is necessary to connect the home of the pupil with the school in the matter of his education. Therefore, the guardians should be properly interested in the education of their wards. Their active co-operation should

be secured to see that the child's study at home is a real continuation of the work done in the school.

(10) Suitable text-books must be provided. This is a matter of the utmost importance. A good deal of the primary education in our country has been spoilt by the use of bad text-books requiring the use of wrong methods of instruction.

(11) There should be a proper correlation of the subjects taught. A great deal of harm is done by teaching the subjects as if these formed separate watertight compartments. It seems that even very few of our teachers really appreciate this point. Special efforts should be made to convince them of its importance.

(12) As character is the foundation of life, character building must have a prominent place in the scheme of education. The influence of the teacher should be the chief factor in moulding the character of the student. Therefore, personality and character in a teacher should be as much sought for and valued as his intellectual qualification. A course of moral and religious instruction should certainly be included in the school curriculum.

If the above points are consistently kept in view, it should be possible to build up a school system which will meet with the needs of our country. Following the example of some European countries, it would be an advantage to have separate schools for children of six to ten, ten to fourteen, and fourteen to eighteen years. But perhaps this is not quite feasible in a poor country like ours, and it will be better to have only two sets of schools for children up to ten to eighteen. In that case, co-education of both boys and girls could be carried on in the elementary schools, and the wide employment of women teachers to conduct them would not only result in some economy, but would also open out to educated women a large avenue of useful and congenial work.

It will be a glorious day for India when universal primary education of the proper type will prevail in the land. Broadbased on this, it will then be possible to rear a sound system of secondary education, culminating in University education of a very high type. It should be so arranged that students who do not wish to go up for University education might be released at the age of fourteen or fifteen with sufficient general education to undergo a special commercial or technical training.

At present with over ninety per cent people locked up in eternal ignorance, many an unknown Handel or inglorious Milton is altogether condemned to blush unseen. Who shall dare to estimate the moral and material advance of India when once the masses are educated, and the best intellects among her vast population are churned up to the top, to guide, lead and serve their motherland? The task is no doubt the mightiest in the world, but its reward will also be the greatest. Then, and not till then, will the full significance of Indian culture and civilisation be manifest to the world and its influence felt by the human race. The nation should, therefore, lend its utmost energies and resources to accomplish this glorious task.

Humanism Through Schools

This is a two-part article. The first part comprises excerpts from a series of articles written by Mr. M.N. Kapur for The Statesman *during 1970-1971. Read together, they articulate his ideas about education. Therefore, this part is called 'Educational Ideas'. The second part by his wife, Amrita Kapur, is about the man M.N. Kapur. It is written as a series of anecdotes which exemplify the ideas expressed in Part I.*

—Editors

I. Educational Ideas

M.N. Kapur

Catch'em Young for Physical Training
16 February 1970

As a member of the Wanchoo Committee, instituted by the Ministry of Education a few years ago, to go into the affairs of the Rajkumari Coaching Scheme, I had suggested that instead of depending only on physical training instructors and highly qualified coaches, all young able-bodied school teachers should go, during holidays, for a short-term training course in a game of their liking and start basic sports training centres in their own schools. Gradually, these courses could be repeated and enlarged for greater efficiency. In this way a school can have even a dozen centres for basic coaching in different games manned by teachers of different subjects and organized by the physical education teacher. A small allowance to the teachers for this additional sports work will pay a richer dividend than a few sophisticated training camps where usually the efficient and the indifferent rub shoulders with each other and attain very little....

Some schools with facilities and some specially planned sports centres can impart advanced training in one or more games and fully qualified coaches can train the basically trained young people and build on what is already there. Several such sports centres with adequate provision for playing fields can be conveniently located in different parts of a town.

Sports Needs a Shake-Up
April 1970

'Scrap the existing sports set-up and start afresh' is the remedy of a senior sports official for raising standards. His views merit consideration for it is obvious that all is not well with our sports organizations and with our standards. It is equally obvious that the slogan, 'Taking part is more important than winning', is a mere paper slogan these days....

Somehow the Indian Government is always on the defensive, although it spends more public money in sending contingents abroad than many other democratic countries. Even if money is raised by federations and associations it is in the national interest to select and send out the very best team possible. In developed democratic countries, strong public opinion does not allow any selection committee to ignore a deserving sportsman.

The only effective way to improve standards is to organize sports in schools and colleges in a better way and catch our athletes young.

Lack of Ideal Cause of Campus Unrest
8 June 1970

Over two thousand years ago Plato observed, 'What is happening to our young people? They disrespect their elders, they disobey their parents. They ignore the laws. They riot in streets inflamed with wild notions. Their morals are decaying. What is to become of them?'....

This has been more or less true throughout history. There are always two forces acting on human society—'caution' of age and 'daring' of youth. If it is all caution without daring the world would not progress. If, on the other hand, it is all freedom without the sobering influence of age it would be a wild society resulting in survival of the fittest. It has to be a judicious combination of the two....When vested interests under the cover of religion and outdated traditions, control society and the strong exploit the weak there is an upheaval. Youth always spearheads such a change. Today, once again, youth is revolting against age for its exploitation of society....

The two World Wars were the creation of an adult society. This was bound to affect the thinking of children. As if this was not enough, adults have invaded the make-believe world of children by providing them with toy guns, tanks and machine-guns, miniature instruments of destruction....In short, we adults have exploited our own children by supercharging their world with drugs, violence, sex and crime. Behind all this is profit motive of the adult, camouflaged with convenient cover of art and free enterprise of a free society. So let us stop blaming the young for a while for their unusual behaviour and see if we adults are playing our part as parents, teachers and leaders....

Many developing countries have harnessed this by providing challenging tasks for social and educational reconstruction of society. Physical reconstruction, in the form of road-building, land-reclaiming and other construction projects for the community are popular because of the challenge they throw to the youth. But for this, some type of central planning and compulsion, both internal and external, is necessary for success. It is the lack of an ideal and a big enough challenge that produce *senas* and anti-social activities....

What we are witnessing today in college campuses is mainly the result of political parties trying to gain control of tomorrow's voters. It is a struggle for power, and it seems the ends justify the means. Democracy means freedom, almost unlimited freedom, even to destroy oneself. If public leaders of India do not sit together and evolve an ideal and a code of behaviour, misguided youth will create chaos. Maybe some people want this, as out of this chaos emerges a certain type of society. It is unfair to use the youth for our own ends, material or political, and then blame them for what they do. It is for us parents, teachers and public leaders to harness the daring of youth and evolve a fair society for India... .

Vinoba Bhave when asked by a teacher to suggest the best way of making the youth do constructive work remarked: 'Do it yourself and they will follow'. Example is better than precept, is an accepted and oft-quoted proverb.

Physical Education and The Three R's

14 September, 1970

There was a time when education in the three R's—reading, writing and arithmetic—was considered adequate for the young. Activities like art, craft, music, dramatics, first considered extra-curricular, then co-curricular, are now considered an essential part of education itself. Similarly, physical education in advanced countries like Russia, the USA, Germany, Japan and others, is no more extra-curricular or co-curricular activity but an integral part of general education.... Recognition of this fact by educationists has changed the concept of total education. Now, general education is not complete without aesthetic or physical education. When asked to indicate their priority in these three aspects, they said there were no priorities. These were three sides of a equilateral triangle—each as important as the other....

It should be recognized that a high degree of efficiency in competitive sports is not possible without a very high standard of physical fitness and therefore, physical education should be considered an essential part of general education in schools and colleges. The possibility of awarding school and university scholarships to outstanding sportsmen, who are reasonably good students, should be explored.

Guiding The Average Student
16 November, 1970

In any reasonably developed society, persons of very high or very low intelligence and ability would probably constitute about 30% of the total population. The highly intelligent one will, given a reasonable chance, stand out sooner or later. The one with low intelligence can develop only to a certain extent. The bulk of the society, about 70%, range from reasonable to good average intelligence and ability.

While highly intelligent persons will be the philosophers, scientists, scholars, poets and artists, it is the persons with good average intelligence who will man most of the essential services and handle business, trade, commerce, industry and education. Therefore, everything possible should be done to educate this effective majority to develop initiative, courage and confidence. The foundation of this must be laid in the school.

Some average children of professional persons will inherit ambitions from their parents and will get their stimulus to work and achieve something worth while straight from the text-books howsoever dull they may be. In the present social set-up this number may not be large. Most students will require additional encouragement. A good library will help the reading type. The extrovert types will get their boost from debates and elocution. More practically minded need educational projects to fire their imagination.

Games and Sports

A healthy average student will be instinctively interested in games and sports. As in the case of mental development, beyond a certain minimum, the need for physical exercise differs from individual to individual. While cricket may be the requirement of many, kabaddi may satisfy others. As it is not easy to provide many games in one school, games selected should be those which require lesser space and offer varying degrees of challenge to students.

Many average students become difficult when they do not get a legitimate outlet for their physical energy through games. Achievement in games and sports and the appreciation that follows it, not only cures problem cases but develops confidence and courage to meet the challenge of life later. If properly handled, confidence gained in games and sports can help a student do better in studies. This very confidence will help him do better in life later.

A sensitive child of average intelligence will be attracted towards aesthetic activities like art, craft, music, dance and drama. If he gets a chance to express himself through these activities he will develop into a satisfied, confident and a well integrated person capable of achieving much when he grows up.

Good School

Therefore, a good school should have all these activities built in, in its daily routine, so that every student has chance to pick up stimulus suited to his requirements and flower out.

Man is a social animal and likes to live and work in company. Working together requires proper social adjustment. The process of social adjustment starts early in the family and becomes important at the school stage. One thing that stands in the way of proper social adjustment is one's ego. Everybody wants recognition and appreciation.

At the school stage when boys and girls are developing into men and women, the desire for recognition is very great. An unrecognized person either sinks into oblivion or turns a bully. A healthy average boy, specially the extrovert type, who is not fettered by the weight of either extraordinary or inadequate intelligence, is more likely to become extra bold, aggressive or even a bully. His natural exuberance will keep him from going down and getting lost. And hence it is all the more necessary to provide him with opportunities for self-expression and of shouldering responsibility. The first will satisfy his creative instinct and the latter his ego.

There are a few accepted positions of authority in a school, but they are not enough. Ways and means must be found of multiplying these so that as many students as possible can shoulder responsibility. Instead of just one head-boy and one head-girl, there can be several prefects looking after various activities of the school. Then there can be House captains, games and club captains. Instead of one class captain for a year, a system of weekly captainship will provide opportunity of shouldering responsibility to many. The school can be divided into junior, middle and senior and this system of sharing responsibility can be multiplied.

If living together is to be peaceful and satisfying then there must be some rules of social behaviour. As at the senior school stage young boys and girls are bursting into men and women, defiance of rules which means restrictions is natural. Experience has shown that in schools rules are broken by students more because of misunderstanding, inadequate or wrong information than by deliberate and calculated action.

A regular built-in routine of free and informal discussion at different levels clears the air, helps both students and the authorities to understand each other's point of view and creates an informal and friendly atmosphere. In such an atmosphere the need for elaborate set of rigid rules is almost eliminated.

All Alone

When a young, healthy, average boy or a girl comes to a large school for a while, he stands all alone in a big crowd of students, timid and afraid. Different teachers see only the aspect of his personality reflected in the efficiency or lack of it in their own spheres. There must be somebody in the school to take charge of him, stretch him to his limits in studies, sports and aesthetic activities, praise him for his achievement, help him in his problems, respect him as an individual and treat him like a man. Such a person can be the Housemaster—his guardian angel in the school. Care, affection and support of the Housemaster help an average student to gain confidence to do his best in the school and learn to create a place for himself in society.

In democratic countries schools, independent or Government which have harnessed the energies of healthy average individuals, have earned the respect of generations. Let us equip our schools and look after our average students, at least the more promising ones. They are the backbone of the country.

An Investment Long Overdue

15 February, 1971

Now it is realized that proper development and exploitation of natural resources is possible and profitable only when qualified people, such as engineers, technicians, organizers, office workers, are available for the work.... .

So education is now considered an investment in all advanced countries. It is now accepted that a nation's capital is increased whenever a school, a laboratory or a university is opened. In other words, education, which involves expenditure, often heavy expenditure, is also a source of enrichment for the future.... This implies that it is just as important to invest in men as in capital equipment. This realization has aroused the interest of society in education at all levels....

Instead of passing on a certain quantum of knowledge, the teacher must now give his students an interest in continuous learning and an ability to think for themselves and find what they need for their growth and employment in new situations.... What Montaigne said four hundred years ago, that a well-trained head is better than a well-filled head, is truer today than even before....As already stated, education is an investment which involves heavy expenditure. It should be given priority. But should this priority be given to any kind of education? In a society, the wisdom of any investment is judged by what it returns to society. As education in every country, especially a developing one, is going to be one of the biggest and costliest undertakings, it is only fair that its success or failure should be judged by the quality of young men and women it produces. Is our education worth the investment it demands?....

With a new Parliament round the corner, let us hope that our new leaders and parliamentarians will give adequate importance and priority to developing our human resources which alone can make the development of natural resources possible and profitable. Someone has rightly said, 'The future belongs to those nations which turn to the best account the intelligence of their young people—of all their young people'.

The Importance of School Teachers

The question is, are we looking after our teachers as well as we should? If we are then why is there a tremendous shortage of teachers of all categories? How is it that a large majority of parents would not like their children to join this nation-building activity? Again why is it that a large proportion of this nation-building clan is of average ability, if not actual 'rejects' from other professions? If education is the biggest and the most important investment specially in a developing country like India such questions must be faced and answered....

Decline and Fall of the Teacher

26 April, 1971

There was a time when a teacher was a highly respected person in the Indian society. Even a few generations ago he was genuinely respected by society. This respect was born not only of the fact that the teacher knew more than the pupils, but out of the attitude of mind, that a person who helps a near-animal human child to become a civilized and a cultured human being, deserves the respect of both students and society. It was considered a privilege on the part of those in authority to give recognition and social status to the teacher. His status in society was higher than of many highly paid officials... .

The situation has changed now and many factors are responsible for this. A technician, an engineer or a doctor is considered a more useful and hence a more respected member of society as his contribution is quick, direct, visible and mechanically measurable.....

In other words, the intellectual superiority of the teacher has been challenged. His invisible contribution for the betterment of the individual for a better society is not being appreciated enough. Direct and visible material contribution even by lesser qualified persons is attracting more recognition. This has meant lesser importance and therefore lesser pay for teachers. All this has, by and large, bewildered and frustrated the teacher. The fact that, off and on, this injustice by society is recognized by those in power, does not help him. To call him a 'nation-builder' and keep him in poverty, both material and social, on the one hand, condemn black-marketeers on the public platform and give them social prestige and official patronage on the other, has affected the mental attitude of the teacher community... .

Neglect of teachers has, in turn, produced shortage of teachers of both primary and secondary education. In India usually those who are unable to find better jobs come to the teaching profession....As mentioned earlier, in unfair situations in society, automatic adjustments take place, which usually are not in the best interests of society. If society has been unfair to teachers, they too, in turn, have come to do less and less for society. This is to put it mildly. The possibilities of this mutual give and take and adjustments for the benefit of the new generation, have to be examined for quick action as we cannot afford to wait for long now.

Learning Through Science
22 November, 1971

Science, in itself, being pure knowledge, is neither good nor bad. It is the use we make of it that determines its impact on humanity. A knife in a murderer's hand kills; in a surgeon's hand it cures, and in a scientist's hand it explores and creates new knowledge....They say, nowadays, that a book, specially of science, becomes out of date by the time it is published! In his book, *The Library of Living Philosophers*, Albert Einstein says, 'It is in fact nothing short of a miracle that the modern methods of instruction have not yet entirely strangled the holy curiosity of inquiry; for this delicate little plant, aside from stimulation, stands mainly in need of freedom: without this it goes to wreck and ruin without fail. It is a very grave mistake to think that the enjoyment of seeing and searching can be promoted by means of coercion and sense of duty.'

A housewife should be made aware of the use of science, not only as a handy servant but also as an agent for saving time, energy and money. The results of research in the laboratory should be brought to the man in the street so that he may develop materially, socially and culturally... . How can this be achieved? Science Exhibitions if properly planned and executed can make a significant contribution in this direction. By these a specialist or an inventor can be brought in contact with the common man who, in turn, will benefit from the advance made by science. Besides, Science Exhibitions encourage initiative and creative ability.

They provide opportunities to the young to learn from others. They help them to realize that the complicated Principles of Science can easily be explained and understood by simple experiments which they themselves can perform. The preparation of a project for an exhibition puts a young person in the position of an inventor or creator and gives him the feeling of satisfaction....

Planning and organizing successfully an effective science exhibition needs the cooperation of Government, research workers, scientists, science teachers, industry and commerce and other agencies connected directly or indirectly with the propagation of scientific knowledge. One such cooperative effort has resulted in the first science exhibition for children which has been organized in the Capital, planned under the guidance of Dr. D.S. Kothari and sponsored by the Jawaharlal Nehru Fund, National Council of Science Education, National Council of Educational Research and Training and the Bal Bhawan. It has turned out to be an outstanding show. Well over a hundred institutions from all over India have taken part in it to provide over two thousand exhibits ranging from verification of a simple principle of school science by material of everyday use to the display and use of sophisticated apparatus developed or employed in advanced technical institutes....Although it was the first venture, and arrangements will improve by experience, it has succeeded admirably in arousing the interest of students and teachers alike.

Teachers Must Show the Way

14, February 1972

They say the battle of Waterloo was won on the playing fields of Eton and Harrow, implying thereby that the qualities of initiative, confidence, and courage displayed by young officers in this battle were developed through games, sports and other challenging activities during their school career in these or other well - known public schools... . Besides these qualities, schools expect their students to have public spirit and courage to stand for the right cause even if it means facing criticism, difficulty and unpopularity....

There is a saying, that 'The world in which we live are two, the world we think and the world we do'. Unless we teachers subject ourselves to the very discipline we expect from our students as armed forces officers do, we will not get much response from them.... Let us take punctuality. When a school starts in the morning we expect our students to be in their places on time. A student arriving late is reprimanded if not actually punished. Do all teachers reach the school or their classes in time?...

Sometime a teacher has to punish to help the student develop on the right lines. This is a painful process and should make a teacher unhappy. Do we all feel that way?.... They say 'Habits start as cobwebs and end in chains'. If we want our students to develop good habits, stand up for justice and fairplay, and do their duty in face of difficulty and criticism, then we will have to show them how to do this by our own example. There is no other way.

II. Tales of MNK

Amrita Kapur

Mayo

In 1933, the Principal of Mayo College, Stowe, asked Garrett, the Principal of Government College, Lahore, to recommend some one outstanding for a teaching post in his institution—preferring a science graduate and a sportsman. This is not a usual combination. Science students generally do not have time for sports since science practicals are held after classes. Garrett asked M.N. who decided to go to Ajmer, to see Mayo and assess for himself. He was twenty-three years at that time. I am told that Stowe was sitting in front of the school pavilion when he first set eyes on M.N. He liked M.N. and straightaway asked whether he would join and when could he start? Just out of college with an M.Sc. degree, there were no plans afoot, so M.N. thought 'Why not?' The appointment was under the category 'Indian Master' for teaching science and sports. Starting pay, I think, was Rs. 200 or even less! Thus started a teaching career, which uninterruptedly continued for half a century. The 'English Masters' were few, the 'Indian Masters' many. 'Indian Masters' were second class citizens. I shall narrate a few incidents which mark M.N. as an extraordinary member of staff.

The English Masters' pay grades were around four to five time higher than of the Indians. The English received their pay by cheques and the Indians in cash, standing in a queue in front of the office. M.N. resented this. 'Give us our pay through cheques—be it one-fourth theirs, or less. We shall not line up to receive it.' An Indian Master said to him: '*Hamey to jharu par bhi rakh kar denge to ley lenge*' ('If they place it on a broom and give it to us we will accept it'). M.N. did not relent and the pay-cheque system was established.

Another incident. Once an English guardian of a prince was riding a horse inside the college campus—exercising. M.N. was passing that way and the guardian started discussing his ward with him. Riding on, he expected the Indian Master to walk along and continue the talk. M.N. stopped and said, 'Mr. Housen, either you stop your horse and then talk to me, or we shall meet another time'. Housen never forgot this and was vengeful for the rest of the time in Mayo!

It was one of the traditions in Mayo to have a Garden Party after the Annual

Day function. The invitees were divided by a rope boundary into an English guests and Princes enclosure, and an Indian guests enclosure. M.N. was made in-charge of the function. It must have happened for the first time in the history of this princely institution that the barrier was removed and it became one gathering of all the guests. The Principal was aghast.

Theatre was a new experience when M.N. was put in charge. He decided to use a Rajput theme and setting. A play, *Maharana Pratap* was staged. It was an open-air performance. Horses were brought on to the stage, swords were got out of the armouries of the Raj Kumars. The treatment and theme was novel and unseen in Mayo till then. Another production, *A Pageant on Ajmer* was equally imaginative.

He had taught for three years, when the school inspectors, all Englishmen visiting Mayo College, made an offer to send him for further training in Education after seeing him teach senior classes. Stowe wanted him to go to the Lahore Training College, but M.N. went to the University of London instead.

When Mayo was declared a Public School—transition from a Princes' College—the House system of residence for students was introduced. We were the first to move into residence with the boys and to become their guardians. This was the time when McCanlis from Cheltenham School, England, took over from the more orthodox Stowe. When we left Mayo to come to the Modern School, Delhi—our wards were sitting on the Ajmer House steps, weeping. McCanlis remarked, 'If I received half as much love and regard from my students, I would consider myself a successful teacher.'

Modern

Arrival. In 1947, after fourteen years in Mayo, M.N. came to Modern School to face a new challenge. We all know with what ideals the Modern School's Founder, Lala Raghubir Singh, started the school in 1920. His own dedication, his noble spirit to serve the cause of education by founding a school rich in our national heritage, is by now a legend. We know the school was visited by Gandhiji, Gurudev Rabindranath Tagore, Reverend C.F. Andrews and many such distinguished personalities, who gave inspiration for the goal that Lalaji had set. Idealism was thus the foundation stone of Modern School, a good inheritance for any principal. Equally important for M.N. was the love and regard in which Lalaji held him. M.N. reciprocated that with a full heart.

M.N. came for the interview in June 1947. Sardar Bhagwant Singh narrated the incident during the memorial service for M.N. held in the Senior Modern School on 4 April 1994:

'I remember the day when Mr. Kapur came as a candidate for the post of the Principal of Modern School. There were three or four candidates who were senior to him in age and experience. On just going through the bio-data of the applicants we all thought to ourselves—the cheek of this young man to apply for the post of the Principal of Modern School! But when this young man walked into the room all of us were impressed with Mr. Kapur's personality and bearing. The only thing that was against him was his age and his lack of experience. After the interview was over, we discussed the merits of the candidates. Seasoned and wise men of the world like Sir Sobha Singh, Lala Shri Ram, Mr. Mukherji and Lalaji himself, had no hesitation in saying that Mr. Kapur would be the best choice for the post and he will soon gain in experience what he was lacking in age.'

M.N. happily took up the challenge, although facilities and pay at Modern School were nominal compared to Mayo. But it worked out beautifully indeed. M.N. built the school to the level of an outstanding Public School of post-Independence India.

Continuing Education. In the coming decades, to enrich his own experience, M.N. visited schools of all types in Europe, England and America. His purpose was to learn, to pick up ideas, to blend them into the school culture and curriculum, and thereby, to provide the best to the students. I mean it when I say, to blend, not to replace. I was often with him on these visits. I have met Principals and Headmasters of schools in different parts of the world and I can say with pride that M.N. stood out among the best.

He believed in continually enriching himself on the home front as well, and to pass on the quest to the students. It was from Mayo that he went to Wardha to learn, at first hand, about Gandhiji's Basic Education philosophy. A great experience! While in Modern School, he introduced the students to Vinoba Bhave. Vinobaji was camping in Bulandshahr when we took a batch of students to meet him. We spent the day with him and early next morning, before sunrise, the students walked with Vinobaji learning about his Bhoodan Movement and much more. Mandalsa Behn had organized this for us and it was her mother Shrimati Jamna Lal Bajaj who once addressed the school assembly in the morning. She narrated to the children her life's work with Gandhiji. It was in Jaipur, I think, that Gandhiji, in a gathering, had asked the women to voluntarily donate their gold ornaments, 'shackles' as he called them. Bangles and chains and rings piled up spontaneously in a heap....Morning assembly was the time for this sort of exposure—the world opened beyond school boundaries, beyond school books, beyond Delhi. Intellectuals, artists, men of religion, sportsmen, people from all fields were invited as guest-speakers to give colour and richness to the school curriculum. This was one aspect of exposure and enrichment. The other aspect was practical experience of day to day life. I shall narrate some stories to illustrate this.

A compassionate heart. Once we came across a man with no legs sitting under a tree, in the compound of Hanuman Mandir on Irwin Road. M.N. came back, took some students, and returned to the spot. Immediately they decided to adopt him and brought him to the school. The man perched himself on the platform under the Kathal tree (outside the physics laboratory). His food, clothes, and other requirements were looked after. Then the students got together and presented him with a wheelchair. He propelled himself around in the campus—to the dining hall, to the toilets, to the sports field—wherever. On Diwali Mela—it was being held in the cricket field that year—Mrs. Sonia Gandhi came for a while, as Priyanka and Rahul were in Junior School at that time. This school guest was introduced to her. I consider this a fine example in humane education.

There used to be a tea party before the House Functions which was meant to greet the teachers and to meet the parents. The House in order to save money and use it for a cause, decided to make the tea frugal. They bought blankets with the saved money. We all set out in the school bus after night fall, chose an area, for example, Asaf Ali Road or Daryaganj, and spotting homeless people sleeping on the pavement in the cold, covered them with blankets.

The students started another venture. They collected clothes and other useful articles over a time period and then held a Bazaar in the school campus for helpers' wives and children. The prices were obviously nominal. In the same spirit we invited Amar Kaur Behanji to run a school—first at the swimming pool and then in the workshops—for helpers' children and their mothers. These children learnt enough at this primary level to get entry into regular schools later and the mothers learnt knitting, sewing and other useful ways of life. At Diwali melas, they had an independent stall for their hardwork. Amar Kaur Behanji, who was later placed on a regular pay, retired in due course. She is still remembered for her invaluable contribution.

Another interaction with the school family was epitomized in the tale of Rampal Singh, the typist who was a personality in his own right. Mrs. Nelson, who played the piano and taught singing to juniors, found this frail man sleeping in the verandah of a church. This was right after the Partition. Rampal Singh was homeless, penniless, a refugee who had come to Delhi with his family. Mrs. Nelson told M.N. about this and he offered help. Rampal was asked what he could do. He said he knew typing. So he was given a job, a place to live, his daughters given seats in the school. Above all he was given respect. Such acts mean faith in oneself and faith in the other. It never fails. Rampal Singh proved to be a man quite unique—proud, fearless, and eccentric. Once early in the morning, at about 5 a.m., there were calls from down below our house. 'Kapur Sahib! Kapur Sahib!' M.N. looked out of the window. Rampal Singh stood there with a full-boiled egg in his hand. He said 'Kapur Sahib, I have brought this for you. As soon as I start to eat it, I see your name on it. So it is you who must eat it'. Imagine his trust in M.N. that he would not be rebuffed, nor made fun. of. Here was a bond—a bond which would not create indiscipline, casualness or familiarity, but respect and affection among the school family.

The question of discipline, as always! Gradually discipline was brought to a level where punishment was hardly needed. Students developed the courage to acknowledge their 'mistakes', indeed they did not hesitate to acknowledge them in the morning assembly, with no feeling of humiliation. In fact such a student must have emerged a hero by demonstrating exemplary courage and conduct. So the rod was spared and the child was not spoilt ! Discipline was imposed imperceptibly, not rigidly. The result was a happy growth of an all-round personality.

Behind this achievement was the fact that each child was known personally, each report card was gone through, commented upon and remembered. Each child, along with his family had his unique place. So the bond became lasting.

S-5 leavers were asked to write their views and perceptions of the school. This was a bold decision because they gave frank and open comments—critical, appreciative, prescriptive. It reveals mutual faith developed over many formal and informal encounters. For example, instead of teaching a subject formally just to fulfil requirements of the Education Department, the Principal's period took on a novel feature. All the sections of a class assembled in the hall for this period and students had the freedom to express any of their problems or queries. During one of the school inspections, the inspectors were curious to see this approach of taking a class. At the end of the period they said, 'Mr. Kapur not many Principals would be able to do this. It needs a lot of courage and confidence for both sides to handle something like this.'

Putri Pathshala! The more westernized and snobbish headmasters would often comment, Kapur's Modern School is a *Putri Pathshala*. An Indianization of the daily school routine was introduced with full confidence of the effect. One such routine was the morning assembly. Most morning assemblies at such schools were held either standing outdoors or sitting in chairs inside the halls. In Modern School, the student congregation sat on durries in the hall, cross-legged, (eyes closed I should presume!) singing songs, from Gurudev Rabindra Nath Tagore or a secular poem, or an all-faith bhajan, and then go on to the day's business in school. The atmosphere in the Modern School morning assembly became a serene influence on the young minds. This atmosphere was Indian, national. School functions held at various occasions, were always set within our diverse cultural tradition. So Modern School became a progressive school, a far cry from being dubbed the *Putri Pathshala*.

Mr. Bond. Over time, M.N. earned the name Mr. Bond. For one thing, wherever there was trouble, or chaos, or excitement, he would silently appear on the scene. As he wore rubber soled shoes, he could pad around noiselessly! The other Bond was the man full of genuine and enduring affection.

Sharing the enthusiasm with boys and girls, meant always being present at every match, enthusing the teams. For N.C.C. camps he would go to Poona. He would travel to Patiala to attend events at the sports institute. He would be there at the horse riding shows and swimming meets wherever his students were participating or go on a trek to Rohtang Pass. A sportsman of great merit himself, he loved this school activity and shared with the students as much enthusiasm as was humanly possible.

An exuberant nature with genuine care of his pupils, ability to be one with them, participating in their activities—outdoor and indoor—understanding their needs, these are the qualities of a successful teacher. Rather, they are requisites for a teacher. If they are naturally part of his nature they are made available effortlessly to the children. I would say that M.N. had these qualities in ample measure and therefore became what the children nicknamed him: Bond.

Cyrus Shroff, an eminent eye surgeon today, joined the Kindergarten section of Modern School. On the first day, he was carrying a very heavy bag to the classroom. The Kindergarten was on Barakhamba Road at that time. Cyrus was resting with his heavy bag on the ground, on his way from the main gate to the K.G. block. M.N. was passing that way. He noticed this little scholar, went up to him and asked, is the bag very heavy? Cyrus said, yes it is very heavy. M.N. said, may I carry it for you? Cyrus gladly accepted the offer. The bag and the little Cyrus reached their destination! It was much later that Cyrus came to know who this sweet man was, who carried his bag!

Years later in senior school, in one of Mr. Ved Vyas's Roopaks, Cyrus narrated a couplet of the poet Bismil. M.N. never forgot that moment or the couplet as it epitomized his own approach to life:

Idhar aa sitamgar hunar aazmaaen
Tu teer aazma hum jigar aazmaaen
(Come O Tyrant let us try our skills
You try the bow and arrow, I try my heart.)

Modern School, 24 Daryaganj, 1920

Modern School, Barakhamba Road, 1935

School Staff, 1924

Sitting from left: Udit Mishra, Juthika Bose, Kamala Bose, Miriam Young, Nilima Bose.
Standing from left: Balwant Mishra, Sarada Ukil, Raghubir Singh (in dark suit) and C.P. Chaubey.

School Staff, 1947

Second row from bottom: Raghubir Singh and Kamala Bose sitting in the centre.

School staff marching to the new campus on Barakhamba Road, 4th January, 1933.
Seen in the picture are G.D. Rajpal, Awadh Kishore, Maulvi Shafiuddin Nayyar,
Pandit Bhardwaj, Pandit Ojha, Kamala Bose, Sushila Guniwardhan, Ingeborg Baden-Hausen,
Nilima Bose, Raghubir Singh and Mohiuddin.

School staff march led by Daljit Singh, youngest son of Sir Sobha Singh,
from Daryaganj to the new campus at Barakhamba Road, 4th January, 1933.

Painted mural by Sukumar Bose—Hall of Religions

Saraswati, the Goddess of learning—a prominent part of the school reception.
Sculpture by Ramkinkar Baij (1933), former sculpture teacher of the school.

Rai Bahadur Lala Sultan Singh, President, Board of Trustees, 1920-1930

Sardar Sobha Singh, President, Board of Trustees, 1930-1975

Lala Pratap Singh, President, Board of Trustees, 1975-1993

Maj. Gen. Virendra Singh (Retd.)
President, Board of Trustees, 1993-1997, 2000-2010

Sardar Bhagwant Singh
President, Board of Trustees, 1997-2000

Ashok Pratap Singh
President, Board of Trustees, 2010-2018

Ketaki Sood
President, Board of Trustees since 2018

Board of Trustees—2020

Mrs. Kamala Bose, the first Principal
from 1920 to 1947

Mr. M.N. Kapur, the second Principal
from 1947 to 1977

Mr. P.C. Chowdhry
Principal from 1977-1981

Mr. S.P. Bakshi
Principal from 1982-1996

Mr. R.K. Bhatia
Principal from 1996-2000

Mrs. Lata Vaidyanathan
Principal from 2000-2014

Dr. Vijay Datta
Principal since 2014

H.E. Marchioness of Linlithgow at a musical performance, 1937, with Kamala Bose and Sardar Sobha Singh. Sitting, extreme right, is Raghubir Singh.

Sardar Sobha Singh talks to the architect, F.B. Blomfield (left).
Also in the picture (right) are Sardar Teja Singh Malik and Sardar Narain Singh.

Mahatma Gandhi visits the school, 1935.

Gurudev Rabindranath Tagore addressing students, 1936.
Sitting left to right are Hanuman Prasad, Basant Lal, Teja Singh Malik, N.K. Sen and Shankarlal. Also in the picture are Babu Bala Prasad and Raghubir Singh (first and second from right).

Maria Montessori with M.N. Kapur and Amrita Kapur, 1949.

Founder's Day, 1950. Students perform ballet 'They Live in Shadows'.
Standing left to right: N.K. Bose, S.S. Siddhu, Ved Vyas, M.N. Kapur, C. Rajagopalachari (Governor-General of India), Maulana Azad, G.D. Nayyar, Vinod Chopra and S.L. Ahluwalia.

Dr. Rajendra Prasad, first President of India, at the Founder's Day celebrations, 1951.
Sitting from left are M.N. Kapur, Sardar Sobha Singh and Raghubir Singh.

Founder's Day, 1954. Maj. Gen. Virendra Singh receiving Pandit Jawaharlal Nehru.
Looking on are Bhagwant Singh and M.N. Kapur.

H.E. the Dalai Lama visits the Hall of Religions, 1957.
With him are Kanwal Krishna and M.N. Kapur.

School group with Vinoba Bhave, 1958. *Sitting from left,* Purnima Mehta, Geeta Kapur, Jolly Rohatgi, Anju Sachdeva, Meera Verma, Pradeep Kukreja.
Standing include (second from left) Hardayal, Rajat Narain, Anwar Abbas, Narendra Sharma and Ved Vyas.

I was much pleased to see Modern School. The cleanliness of the school and the purity of its atmosphere is indeed praiseworthy.

15/01/1935 — Mahatma Gandhi

It was unfortunate that owing to my weak health I was unable to inspect the Modern School in all its details as was my intention to do. But what I could see has impressed me greatly and left no doubt in my mind that it is one of the best educational experiments in India having a natural life, growth of its own and therefore helping the young minds to grow in an atmosphere of happiness and background of inspired activities of culture.

28/03/1936 — Rabindranath Tagore

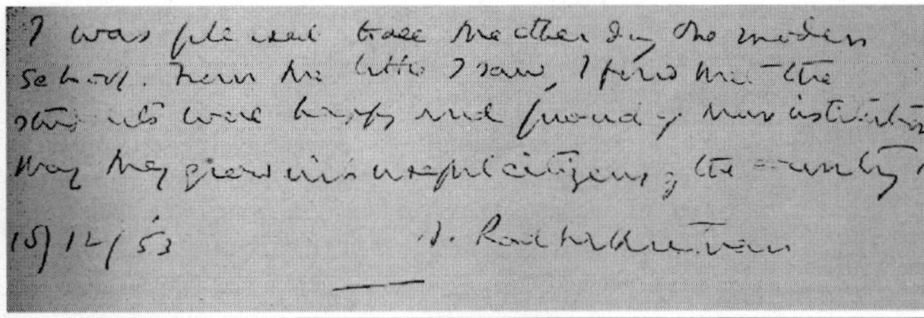

I was pleased to see the other day, the Modern School. From the little I saw, I found that the students were happy and proud of their institution. May they grow up into useful citizens of the country.

10/12/1953 — *Sarvepalli Radhakrishnan*

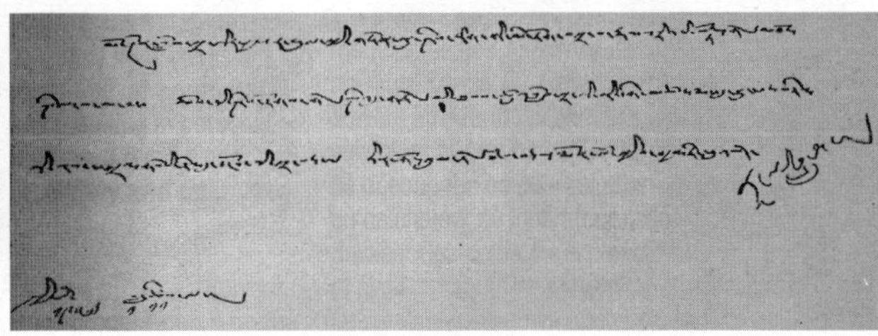

The Modern School not only lets youth of India nurture the myriad flowers of knowledge but also inculcate spiritural wisdom. It is marvelous school of great value. I am gifting my photo as souvenir and Rs. 3000/- with prayers.

11/11/1957 — *Dalai Lama*

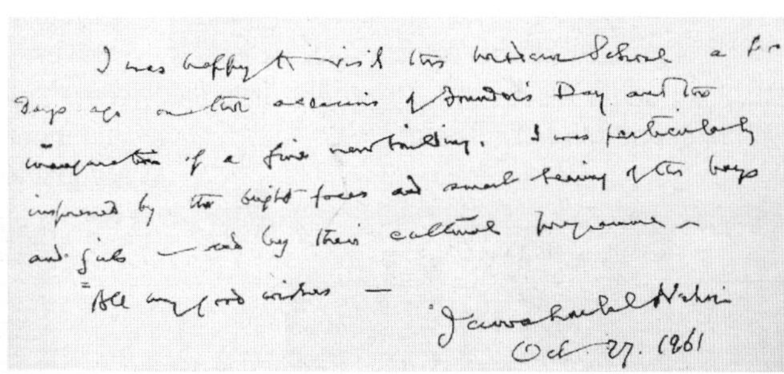

I was happy to visit the Modern School a few days ago on the occasion of Founder's Day and the inauguration of a fine new building. I was particularly inspired by the bright faces and smart bearing of the boys and girls and by their cultural programme. All the good wishes.

27/10/1961 — *Jawaharlal Nehru*

Dr. Zakir Hussain, Vice President of India chatting with Mrs. and Mr. M.N. Kapur, on the occasion of the Founder's Day Celebrations, 1962.

Dr. Karan Singh, Governor of J&K posing with the students after their splendid performance on the occasion of Founder's Day Celebrations, 1965.

The President of India Mr. V.V. Giri arrives for the Golden Jubilee Celebrations, 1970.

Mr. Lal Bahadur Shastri, Prime Minister of India, being escorted by Mr. M.N. Kapur and Mr. Mool Raj Mehndiratta.

Mr. Fakhruddin Ali Ahmed, President of India, with Mrs. and Mr. M.N. Kapur.

Giani Zail Singh, President of India, meeting the members of the Editorial Board of the school Magazine *"SANDESH"*.

Founder's Day 1992 (left to right) Manmohan Singh, S.P. Bakshi, Alice Vari, Mohini Virendra Singh, Anju Pratap Singh and Ketaki Sood.

Dr. A.P.J. Abdul Kalam, President of India with Mrs. Lata Vidyanathan, Mrs. Ketaki Sood and Mr. Bhagwant Singh.

Founder's Day, 1969. Indira Gandhi visits the Art Room. Also in the picture from left are Pooja Rohatgi, Bishamber Khanna, Sujata Sharma, Devayani Kanwal Krishna and M.N. Kapur.

The Gandhis' visit as parents to the Raghubir Singh Junior Modern School, 1978. Indira Gandhi, Sonia Gandhi, Rajiv Gandhi with Savitri Pratap Singh.

Modern School students participating in Republic Day Pageant, 26th January, 1952.

"Shahjehan" staged in 1939.

Founder's Day 1940—Group dance by Students.

Sushil Anand and Syeda Saiyidain in a scene from the first Modernites production *Kanjoos*, directed by Ved Vyas, 1960.

Founder's Day ballet *Muktadhara* directed by Narendra Sharma, 1961. Seen in the picture are Nilima Dhanda, Praveen Puri and Purnima Mehta.

A scene from *Jesus Christ Superstar* with Rohan Aggarwal in the lead role, 1994.

Glimpses from Cultural Activities

Glimpses from Cultural Activities

Music class in progress

The School Orchestra at Founder's Day celebration

Ustad Amjad Ali Khan, student of Modern School,
playing Sarod in his school days

(Above) Sardar Swaran Singh coaching a gymnast.

(Top right) Sports Day, 1958. Oath-taking ceremony—Ganesh Prasad and Ina Dhanda. On the extreme left are Shubhendra Shankar and Ravi Kapoor.

(Centre right) Sports Day, Modern School, Vasant Vihar, 1993. K.J. Vari awarding a prize to Sabrina Madan.

(Bottom right) Taekwondo students of the Raghubir Singh Junior Modern School.

Sprint

Hurdle

Horse Riding

We learn to play with fire

Get...set...go...

Hockey

Football

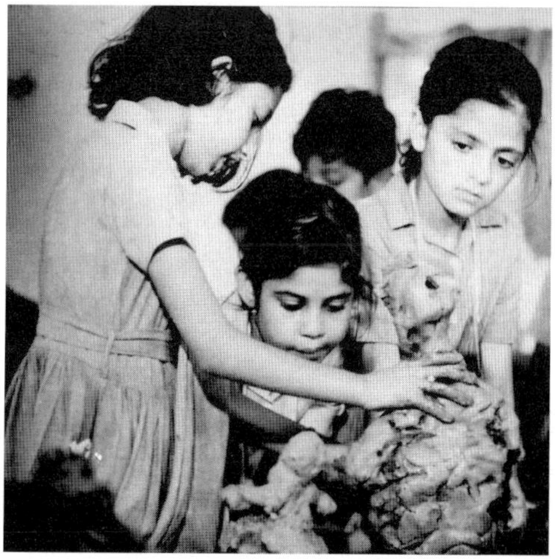

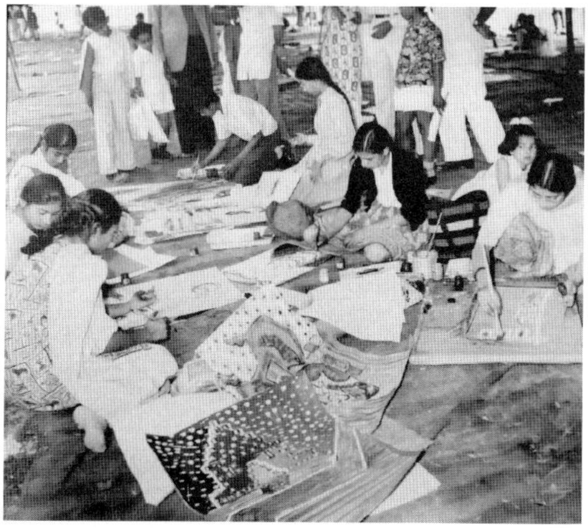

Co-Curricular Activities

Imposing School Building

The Banayan Tree in the School campus,
representing stability and firmness of character

The Platinum Jubilee Block

School Auditorium

Raghubir Singh Junior Modern School

Modern School, Vasant Vihar

Centenary Celebration Archives of Modern School

100 years highlights with School Model in front

School Staff—Centenary Year

Time's Wingéd Chariot

Andrew Marvel, the seventeenth century poet inspires this title:

But at my back I always hear
Time's wingéd chariot hurrying near:

Seventy-five years are difficult to encapsulate in a calendar of events. Every event that occurred revealed its significance much later in the unfolding of the future. We selected a few events to give a sense of how the seventy-five years moved and moulded Modern School.

— *Editors*

1920

August. The Modern School Society is registered under *The Societies Act 1860*. The school opens on 20 October at 24 Daryaganj with six children.

Miss Kamala Bose is appointed Principal.

Syllabus is drawn by the Education Sub Committee: Raghubir Singh, Rattan Lal, C.H.C. Sharp, N.K. Sen, Kamala Bose, Pandit Har Narain Shastri, Maulvi Abdul Rahman.

1921

28 April. An application is made to the Government of India for a site in New Delhi.

1922

A Montessori teacher from England, Miss Scott, is invited to teach in the Montessori section.

1923

The Civil and Military Gazette, Lahore, publishes an article on 20 February. 'The Modern School, An Interesting Educational Experiment.'

1924

> *13 November.* Mahatma Gandhi visits the school. His words pass into history: I was very happy to see this modern institution. The cleanliness of the school is worthy of praise. I have only one fear. If in the flush of the modern, the ancient is lost it would greatly harm the young girls and boys. I take the liberty of saying this because I see the purity of motive in the inception of this school and I want this institution to progress.

The school receives the first government grant of Rs. 1500 per annum.

1926

The school's scouts win the Chief Commissioner's flag.

1927

The Board of Secondary Education gives recognition to the school.

Principal Kamala Bose attends the New Education Conference at Locarno, Switzerland.

Due to the popularity of the Montessori section and to improve accessibility, for students, the Management Committee decides to reduce fees.

1928

The first Rudra Prize is awarded to Bhagwant Singh. The prize is named after Sushil Kumar Rudra, Principal St. Stephen's College, one of the earliest proponents of the school. It is given to the most outstanding student of the year, combining character with learning.

Acting Chief Commissioner, J.N.G. Johnson recommends to the Government of India, the school's application for a plot of land in New Delhi.

1929

The first school trips are taken to places outside Delhi. Senior boys are taken to Amritsar, Lahore, Pindi and Taxilla. Juniors to Rajputana, Jaipur, Ajmer and Chittorgarh.

1930

3 June. Lala Sultan Singh, first President of the Board of Trustees, passes away. He is succeeded by Sir Sobha Singh.

After prolonged negotiations between the Trustees and the Government of India, with the help of Sir Girja Shankar Bajpai, Member Education, the present site on Barakhamba Road, covering twenty-five acres of land, is handed over to the school. The lease is registered on August 4.

A committee is formed to examine the working of the school and suggest improvements. Its members are S.N. Mukerji, Principal St. Stephen's College, Reverend C.B. Young, St. Stephen's College, and Rai Bahadur N.K. Sen, Registrar Delhi University.

1931

Messrs C.G. and F.B. Blomfield are engaged as architects. The foundation is laid on 24 August. All Trustees, staff and students place a brick each to signify the joint effort. Construction begins under the close supervision of Sardar Sobha Singh. In November the Montessori wing moves to the new premises and classes begin in tents.

1932

The western wing is completed in May and the Montessori section moves into the new building. The main ground floor structure is completed in August.

1933

4 January. The whole school including members of the Management Committee, the staff, old students, and the entire student body led by Daljit Singh, youngest son of Sardar Sobha Singh, marches in a procession from Daryaganj to the premises on Barakhamba Road.

1934

24 October. Old students are invited for the first time to commemorate the fifteenth year of the founding of the school.

Students collect Rs. 500 for the Bihar Earthquake.

Students work through the entire summer to construct their own toolshed. Right from digging the foundations, to the roofing and plastering of the structure, they accomplish the entire task.

1935

The school building is completed.

13 January. Mahatma Gandhi visits the school.

28 February. The foundation stone for the gymnasium is laid by a prominent Delhi businessman and philanthropist Lala Hanuman Prasad, the gym is named Lala Chunni Lal Gymnasium, after his father.

Rai Bahadur Baisakha Singh builds the riding school stables.

Chand Prakash stands first in the High School Examination.

1936

28 March. The Hall of Religions is inaugurated by Gurudev Rabindranath Tagore. The fresco on the wall depicts men and women of all religions and nationalities going towards the 'Light of Truth'. The artist is Sukumar Bose of the school art department. Books of all religions are placed there for the students to browse through. It is a meditation room.

The seniors are divided into four Houses, Asoka, Akbar, Shivaji and Tagore. A separate House for girls is Laxmi. Each House is responsible for cleanliness of a portion of the school building. The House Captains are to ensure that the school rules are observed by the members.

1937

2 February. Her Excellency, Marchioness of Linlithgow performs the opening ceremony of the gymnasium and the swimming pool. The funds for the construction of the swimming pool have been provided by the government and Lala Shankar Lal, Secretary, Delhi Cloth and General Mills.

February. Sir Kikabhai Premchand donates to the school a sanitorium named Lady Kikabhai Sanitorium.

3 July-19 July.

The Deccan Tour is the first major trip organised by the school.

November. The New Education Fellowship members visit the school.

December. A sports pavilion is gifted to the school by Maneklal Premchand.

1938

13 December. Sir John Sargent, Educational Commissioner, visits the school, attends the monthly 'social hour' with the children. 'A good building does not necessarily mean a good school', and writes in the Visitor's Book: 'But so far as I could judge from a comparatively short visit, everyone seemed to be taking advantage of the exceptionally fine environment in which they find themselves. There seemed to be a conscious purpose and a concentrated effort about this school which would convince even a sceptic who has watched many vaunted educational experiments go up in smoke, that here, at any rate something of real value is in the process of emerging.'

1939

January. Staff and students put up a variety show for scholarships for deserving students and raise Rs. 1000.

Students participate in an All-India Jambooree held in Delhi which is addressed by the founder of the Boy Scouts Movement, Lord Baden-Powell.

23 December. A scout camp is held at Jarcha.

1940

June. The Delhi Olympics Association and Punjab Swimming Championship is held at Lahore. The school wins several prizes.

1944

Eighth class is started.

1945

In its twenty-fifth year the school has a total enrolment of 334 students.

1947

6 February. Mrs Sarojini Naidu inaugurates the exhibition of children's art.

Miss Bose retires after having served the school for twenty years.

1 November. Mr. M.N. Kapur joins the school as Principal.

1948

Miss Kamala Bose dies in Calcutta.

Sandesh, the school monthly magazine is launched.

1949

9 March. Dr. Maria Montessori visits the school, and inscribes the following words in the Visitors' Book.

> My visit to Modern School in New Delhi has left me with an impression that this is not just a school but a splendid example of modern education. Furthermore, it has developed as a centre for education of the future with a system of instruction which is in keeping with the present world.

29 August. National Cadet Corps starts with Sardar Swaran Singh as instructor. First NCC camp held in December at Khanjhawla.

1950

Last time that the school annual magazine *Adarsh* is published in four languages—Hindi, Urdu, Bengali and English. After this issue, Urdu and Bengali are dropped.

September. The school holds a Mock Parliament with a Question Period about school affairs.

School wins the Inter-School Music Competition.

1951

The Founder's Day Exhibition moves to the main building.

1952

Jawaharlal Nehru visits the school on Founder's Day.

26 January. School participates in the Republic Day celebrations for the first time.

Kindergarten's own weekly *Sandesh* starts.

School starts a psycho-medical clinic.

1 October. 'Young Farmer's Club' is formed. Three-quarter acre of land is allotted to the club which is used by students to learn about farming.

1953

A group of students leave with the Principal for an educational tour of Europe.

A Charity Bazaar is held in aid of school servants.

1954

October. School trips are thrown open to Junior school children.

November. School trip goes to Ceylon.

Kavya Kala Sangam is established and it holds a seminar on children's theatre.

1955

26 January. The school presents the pageant 'Conquest of Everest' at the Republic Day Parade.

The NCC camp is held at Hyderabad. The best troop banner is won for the fourth year.

1956

10 January. 'A red letter day for the school'—revision of salaries of teachers.

2 December. Railway Club is added to the list of hobbies.

The school wins the Delhi State-Inter School Tournament General Championship, by winning cricket, gymnastics, athletics. swimming and water-polo.

The Board of Trustees decides to forego the government grant. With the approval of parents, the fees are raised.

Various Educational Boards are formed—Board of Education (for syllabus), Board of Educational Methods and Library, Board of Backward and Bright Children, Board of Community Service and Student Service Board.

Vocational Guidance Board is formed and aptitude tests are introduced.

1957

Dalai Lama visits in the Hall of Religions where prayers of all denominations are held every Thursday.

Scholarship scheme continues with current offering of seventy-five scholarships.

11 August. The Historical Society celebrates the centenary of the 1857 uprising.

10 September. An International Evening is celebrated and children of various nationalities are invited.

December. The Motor Mechanics Club is started with the donation of an old Ford V8 (convertible) by a parent.

1958

10 October. Lala Raghubir Singh lays the foundation stone for the Junior Modern School at Humayun Road.

The Prefect Room is created.

Students undertake *Padayatra* with Acharya Vinoba Bhave.

1959

26 October. The founder of the school Lala Raghubir Singh passes away.

The number of Prefects is increased from three to five, to give students greater participation in school administration.

Kavi Sammelan and Mushaira are jointly held.

1960

Sarod recital on Founder's Day by twelve-year old Amjad Ali Khan .

Modernites (old students) stage their first play *Kanjoos*, an adaptation by Hazrat Awara, of Moliere's *L'Avare*, directed by Mr. Ved Vyas. A tradition of theatre for entertainment is established.

1961

July. Raghubir Singh Junior Modern School moves to Humayun Road. It is formally inaugurated in October by Prime Minister Jawaharlal Nehru.

Mr. N.K. Bose is appointed the headmaster.

July. Two students are selected to represent India at a youth camp in Artek, U.S.S.R.

1962

January. 'Alok' a movement for moral and spiritual enlightenment and self-improvement is inaugurated.

October. History Society starts a series of talks to observe the Bahadurshah Zafar Centenary.

Work on a Multi-Purpose Hall donated by Sardar Sobha Singh commences. A covered capacity for 1,000 and open seating for 3,000 is proposed.

1964

Uljhan, a play by Boarding House students is staged in aid of the Mayor's Flood Relief Fund.

15 November. An exhibition 'Education for International Understanding' is held. Students' displays on many countries of the world are presented.

Students buy paintings for the school art gallery from the sale proceeds of their own art works.

1965

Kiran Seth Memorial Prize is instituted for the best sportsman of the year. Kiran Seth was killed in action in 1965 in the Sialkot sector.

Hemant Luthra stands first in the Board Examination.

Board of Trustees allocates Rs. 40,000 per annum to provide rent free accommodation to teachers on the school campus.

1966

Anil Sood, Navin Kapur and Saurabh Kumar stand first, second and third respectively in the All-India-Higher Secondary Examination.

1967

Gratuity scheme for all staff. Scales of pay revised.

Modernites Scholarship Fund is instituted by MSOSA (Modern School Old Students' Association) to enable deserving and needy students to acquire a Modern School education.

Kapil Malhotra stands first in the Board Examination.

1968

Introduction of General Knowledge Competition.

The foundation stone of Sir Shankar Lal Hall is laid by the Prime Minister, Mrs. Indira Gandhi. It is proposed as a multi-purpose complex and is donated by Sir Shankar Lal's daughter, Mrs. Savitri Pratap Singh.

A new type of Progress Card is introduced for the Junior School containing the whole year's record of the student.

1969

Nursery and Kindergarten renamed Elementary School.

Amitabh Mukerji stands first in the All-India Higher Secondary Examination.

23 May. News reading at the Morning Assembly starts at the Junior School.

Principal Kapur receives the title Padmashri from the President of India.

Four Houses in Junior School named after flowers—Champa, Moulseri, Gulmohar, Neel Kamal.

For the fourth year, the School wins the Nehru flag *Jai Pataka* for excellence in inter-school sports. It is awarded by the Delhi Schools Sports Board.

1970

In the year of the Golden Jubilee, the enrolment stands at 1400.

President of India V.V. Giri, inaugurates Sir Shankarlal Hall.

Deepak Sethi stands first in the Higher Secondary Examination.

Students in Community Service collect Rs. 13,000 and two television sets to donate to Leprosy Homes.

Construction of the new Boarding House commences.

1971

Rajesh Nandan Pande stands first in the Board Examination.

A photographic exhibition 'Fifty Years of Modern School' is held.

1972

Mrs. A. Sachdeva takes over as Principal of the new Modern School, Vasant Vihar. The school is to be housed in Humayun Road and classes are to be held in the afternoon until the new building is ready.

1973

Sports Club donates Rs. 8,000 to the National Defence fund.

1974

The new Boarding House is completed.

1975

24 January. Foundation stone is laid for Modern School, Vasant Vihar. It moves to its new premises on 21 July. Mr. Ved Vyas is appointed Principal.

1976

15 December. Sir Sobha Singh, President of the Board of Trustees, retires after being associated with the school for fifty-seven years. He is succeeded by Mr. Pratap Singh.

1977

Mr. M.N. Kapur retires.

1978

Rs. 20,000 collected for flood victims of Delhi

1979

18 April. Sir Sobha Singh passes away.

Sir Sobha Singh Block for senior classes starts functioning.

1980

Olympic size swimming pool is inaugurated by Justice Prakash Narain.

1981

September. Raghubir Singh Junior Modern School is bifurcated from Modern School, Barakhamba Road.

Mrs. D. David assumes independent charge of Raghubir Singh Junior Modern School.

1982

Mr. S.P. Bakshi is appointed Principal of Modern School, Barakhamba Road.

Three students get the Rector's Prize at the Delhi University.

August. Eighteen students of Class XI and Class XII leave for Dehradun on a cycling expedition.

September. General Virendra Singh, after having served for twenty-three years, hands over charge of Honorary Secretary, Board of Trustees, to Ashok Pratap Singh.

1983

Interact Club, under the auspices of the Rotary Club is started for social service activities.

Hobbies like gardening, ikebana, sewing as well as journalism and typing are introduced.

1984

November. The Shakespearean Society is founded with the opening production, *Merchant of Venice.*

Raghubir Singh Junior Modern School parents introduce 'read aloud' programme for Classes I and II.

Child Counsellor appointed in the Junior School.

1985

With the help of the PTA, two computers are installed. Two teachers attend the requisite computer course in the National Council for Educational Research and Training.

April. The first senior school short story competition is held in English and in Hindi.

The first Inter-School Quiz Competition is organised by the Quiz Club.

Week-long Science Festival is held by the Science Club with the participation of twelve schools.

The scholarship scheme, instituted to enable the meritorious but needy students to acquire a Modern School education, stands at 100 full scholarships, 10 half scholarships. 40 merit scholars of the Government of India are on the school rolls.

1986

For the first time, computers are offered as a subject.

Rs. 56,000 are raised by the Junior School towards the purchase of an ambulance and donated to the St. John's Ambulance Brigade.

The Junior School holds its Silver Jubilee celebrations at the Siri Fort Auditorium and presents the ballet 'Sone ki Chidiya'.

31 July. Mr. Ved Vyas retires as Principal, Modern School, Vasant Vihar. He is succeeded by Mr. K.J. Vari.

1987

Measures are taken to enhance the security of the school premises. Identity cards are issued to students.

Junior School introduces a two-week Summer Recreation Camp for Classes III, IV and V.

1988

Interact Club activities are enlarged to include visits to Blind School to read to the students, sale of CRY cards and visits to Cheshire Home (for the mentally handicapped) in Okhla.

Vinod Dikshit Foundation, (Vinod, class of 1952, died 1987) institutes a fund for the support of innovative and original projects proposed by students.

Leadership camps for Classes IV and V to identify talent in various fields.

1989

Out of sixty-seven students who appear for Medical entrance examination, thirty are selected.

Red Cross gives a trophy to the school for the highest number of blood donors.

Interact Club receives Best Club award for involvement in community work.

K. Mahindra Education Trust institutes five awards of Rs. 5000 each for students securing first positions in Grades IX, X and XI.

1990

The school hosts the Indian Public Schools' Conference Golden Jubilee celebrations.

Sandeep Bhandari conquers 17,600 ft mountain peak in the Nehru Centenary Boys' Mountaineering Expedition.

Indian Oil Corporation gives Rs. 1 lakh to the Modern School Scholarship Fund.

Oct. 14. Mrs. D. David, Headmistress of the Junior School passes away in New Delhi.

1991

January 1. Ms Geeta Dudeja is appointed Headmistress of the Junior School.

Taekwondo training introduced for Classes I-III.

Computer training introduced for Classes III-V.

Air Chief Marshal S.K. Mehra (Modernite) presents a Hunter aircraft to the school.

Trophy instituted by the Air Chief Marshal for a student who shows exemplary display of courage, initiative and adventure.

Hundred blankets and seven quintals of cloth collected and rushed to Tehri Garhwal for the earthquake victims.

Interact Club adopts a handicapped child.

1992

First Annual Inter-School debate held under the auspices of MSOSA.

Ustad Bismillah Khan gives a lecture-demonstration.

1993

11 October. Mr Pratap Singh, President Board of Trustees passes away. Maj. Gen. Virendra Singh becomes President.

28 October. Savitri Pratap Singh Kindergarten Block inaugurated by Mrs. Mohini Virendra Singh.

1994

30 March. Mr. M.N. Kapur passes away in New Delhi.

20 October. School enters the Platinum Jubilee Year.

The musical, 'Jesus Christ Superstar', is presented at Siri Fort by students of Modern School, Barakhamba Road.

An exhibition of works of art of all the past and present art teachers of the school is held at AIFACS., New Delhi.

Meenakshi Pahuja creates a record by receiving over 500 medals in swimming. She breaks one hundred and fifty records during her school career.

Ballet 'Mukhantar' presented by Narendra Sharma, the school's former dance guru, as part of the Platinum Jubilee celebrations.

1995

Resource Centre started in the Junior School.

Five thousand students enrolled in the three branches as compared with a total enrolment of six students in 1920.

2000

- Renovation of the old Gym.
- Inauguraton of M.N. Kapur Hall.

2002

- Inauguration of Teacher Resource Centre.

2003

- Inauguration of H.L.L. Auditorium.

2004

- Ms Lata Vaidyanathan was decorated with the 'National Award to Teachers—2003'.
- Mr. Ashok Pratap Singh was decorated with the 'Delhi Ratna Award'.
- Organised First Inter-School Invitational Squash Tournament 'Mohini Virendra Singh Trophy'.

2005

- Introduction of Smart Classrooms—Class S1 to S3.

2006

- First International Summit organised on 'Community Development and Leadership Summit' (CDLS).

2007

- Canteen (Fast Trax) Area was constructed.

2009

- Inauguration of 'Tapovan', the Amphi Theatre.

2010

- Inauguration of the 'Golf Academy'.
- The 'Kamala Bose Award' for outstanding research beyond classrooms was institutionalized.
- The 'Sardar Bhagwant Singh Award' for Excellence in Research initiated.

2013

- Air-conditioning of Sir Shankar Lal Hall.

2014

- Football Field high mast lights were installed in the Football Field (supported by MSOSA).
- Re-introduced the Horse Riding in School after a gap of 32 years.
- Inauguration of the Science Park.

- Under the guidance of Ms Ambika Pant, an Archives Building was set up to display 6000 photographs as the archives of Modern School.
- The School's first ever 'Time Capsule' was buried in the School's ground.

2015

- Tennis legends—Mr. Tim Henman, Former World No. 4 and Mr. Goran Ivanisevic, Wimbledon Champion visited the School and conducted a sports clinic for students.

2016

- The 'First Pradeep Virendra Singh Delhi State Open Badminton Ranking Championship' was conducted by the School.
- 'Vijayanta', an Army Tank, was added to the grandeur of the School.

2017

- Ms Carolina Marin, World and Olympic Badminton Champion from Spain visited the School and conducted a Master Class for students.
- Rooftop Solar Energy Project was installed on the roof of the P.J. Block in School.
- Admiral Sunil Lanba PVSM, AVSM, ADC, Chief of the Naval Staff, working chief of the Armed Forces visited the School as the Chief Guest for the Independence Day Celebration.
- Dr Vijay Datta was decorated with the 'National Award to Teachers—2016'.
- Inauguration of six international standard acrylic Tennis Courts and one Grass Court.

2018

- Canadian Prime Minister, Mr Justin Pierre James Trudeau visited the School.
- Mr Kapil Dev and Mr Azharuddin, former Captains of the Indian Cricket Team played a few shots with Dr Vijay Datta, Principal, staff and students and also delivered some insightful tips and trivia about the game.
- General Bipin Rawat, UYSM AVSM YSM SM VSM ADC, Chief of the Army Staff, working chief of the Armed Forces visited the School as the Chief Guest for the Independence Day Celebration.
- Initiation of the Vertical Garden.
- Seven Rain Harvesting Pits were built in School.
- An Audio Recording Studio was set up in the School.

2019

- 'Award of Leadership' to Dr Vijay Datta in the British Parliament, London, United Kingdom.

- Unveiling of the Modern School's Centenary Logo.
- Air Chief Marshal Birender Singh Dhanoa, PVSM AVSM YSM VM ADC, Chairman, Chief of Staff Committee and the Chief of the Air Staff, working chief of the Armed Forces visited the School as the Chief Guest for the Independence Day Celebration.
- 'Global Membership of the Round Square' awarded to Modern School during the 'RSIC 2019'. The Round Square is a consortium of 50 nations. One of the ideals being creativity which is displayed in the symbol stating Round Square promotes out of the box thinking.
- Centenary Sports Day celebration witnessed participation of students of all the branches of Modern School. Mr Kapil Dev, Former Captain of Indian Cricket Team graced the occasion as the Chief Guest.

2020

- 3 Air Quality Index Reading Machines/Monitors were installed in the School.
- Dr Vijay Datta, Principal, was honoured with the 'King Constantine Medal', on behalf of the School, during the Round Square Heads Symposium held in London, United Kingdom.
- Launch of 'Cycle Polo' as a sport in School.

The Memory

The point has been made more than once....that there is often a divergence between the point of view of the boy at school, and the man looking back in retrospect; an implication that men tend to forget, and that it is one thing to regard school from afar and quite another to take a balanced view when Flashy (nickname of a school boy) has you by the neck.

— From *The World of the Public School*
by George Macdonald Fraser

From The Oldest Modernite

Bhagwant Singh

The Platinum jubilee year of the Modern School equals seventy-five years of my association with this school. My family had just migrated to Delhi. We came from a distant desert village-Hadali, about 120 miles west of Lahore. My grandfather Sujan Singh and·my father Sobha Singh were entrepreneurs. Looking back, I admire their enterprising spirit and hard work they put in to make their lives and the future of their families a success story. My father Sobha Singh came to Delhi in 1911 and then decided that his future lay in this city. He met Lala Sultan Singh, a leading businessman of Delhi, in 1915. They admired each other's enterprising approach to life and became close friends. When Lala Raghubir Singh, Lala Sultan Singh's son, decided to start a progressive school on the lines of an English Public School, his father accepted his son's decision and helped him by giving a large house (a sprawling place on approximately 10 acres of land) in Daryaganj to turn it into a school. This two-storey building was large enough to have about twenty class rooms, a dining hall, and a kitchen. There were four sets of rooms for staff, and a large bed cum sitting room for the Principal, Miss Kamala Bose. The grounds were large enough to play football and hockey and for athletics. To give a practical shape to an idealist's dream, Lala Sultan Singh requested Sobha Singh to become a Trustee, with him as President of the School Trust.

When the school opened, it had about fifteen children. The eldest group was about eight years old. I was one of them. Miss Kamala Bose was the Principal and also the maths teacher. She had such a powerful personality that she had only to stare at an unruly student to make him quiet and submissive. Lalaji (Raghubir Singh) taught us English, History and Photography. There were half-a-dozen other teachers including Sarada Ukil, then the most famous artist in India. He designed the school crest. Mr. Ukil also doubled as music teacher and we learnt to sing some Bengali songs.

Society's reaction at the time to the concept of a co-educational school which emphasized the all-round development of the child, was typified by my grandfather's reaction when he came to the first annual day function of the school in 1922. The school had put up an English drama 'Robin Hood' to impress the audience with its English speaking children. Also on display were the children's art and craft works. Students displayed their musical ability by playing various instruments like the esraj, sitar, tabla and violin and singing a couple of songs. One song was Iqbal's 'Sarey Jahan Se Achcha Hindostan Hamara' and another was a Bengali song 'Ogo Dakhin Hawa'. The school report was read out by the Principal. My grandfather could not understand what a woman was doing in a boy's school. He was outraged to see boys playing the sitar and violin! He was furious with my father for his so-called 'advanced ideas'. In rustic Punjabi, difficult to translate, he roundly berated him for turning his grandsons into 'mirasis' and 'Hijras' (roughly translated as minstrels and eunuchs) by subjecting them to such a feminine atmosphere. He was so disgusted by the whole thing that he left Delhi for good to set up an equally profitable empire in cotton ginning factories and farms in Punjab. The reaction was also typical of other parents who started doubting the wisdom of putting their children in such a school.

The school started as a co-educational institution with three girls. This was not only a radical departure from the English Public School system, but was also unlike the Indian concept of education where boys and girls studied in different institutions. Lalaji's concept of education did not distinguish between boys and girls; it was an education for all. His other most important belief was in the all-round development of the child's personality. He laid great emphasis on this by introducing hobbies for children. The school had a photography club, a first aid course and classes in carpentry, gardening and cooking. Music and art were part of the school curriculum from the beginning. Games like hockey, football and basketball were compulsory. All these activities were part of the school's daily routine. It had to therefore be a whole day school. We all lunched together in the school dining hall, followed by one hour's rest period. We were away from home from 8 a.m. to 6 p.m. It was early dawn when we left for school and it was lighting up time when we left school to return home. Everybody—both the students and the teachers—had to arrange their own transport. Most of us came on horse drawn carriages (tongas). As we grew up, we acquired bicycles.

Athletics and drill were a part of our daily routine. We had a Sergeant called 'Dippy' a highlander from a Scottish regiment, who came from the Delhi Red Fort (where his regiment was posted) to teach us marching—military style and drill as in the army. He was a very tall man and loved children. We in turn became very fond of him.

Scouting was another activity that brought the school into the limelight; both amongst other Delhi schools and society. Mr. Raja Ram, who was then a teacher in Modern School (later he became professor and then the Principal of St. Stephen's College), laid the foundation of this movement . He was ably assisted by Mr. Nausher Kapadia who had been an ardent boy scout leader in his school days.

He became a dentist. The Delhi Boy Scouts Association used to hold annual comps during Christmas and New Year holidays. About fifteen Delhi schools used to join this camp and compete in various skills like first aid, signalling, cooking, scout pace, etc. At night, around a bonfire we sang songs, performed skits and other items of entertainment. This counted towards choosing the best Scout Patrol.

The Modern School had two Scout Troops competing. I was the proud head of one of the Scout Patrols. We won the maximum points in the camp and won the Scout Flag, the top prize, year after year. We never lost this prestigious prize in all the years that the Scouts movement existed. A press photograph by the Boy Scouts giving the guard of honour to the then Viceroy Lord Willingdon, accompanied by Sir Sobha Singh, was published in the newspapers.

Another aspect of education Lalaji exphasized was trips to historical sites. We had day trips to monuments, in and around Delhi and trips of longer duration to places like Agra, Fatehpur Sikri, Benares, Bodhgaya, Patna, Jaipur, Udaipur, Chittor, Ajmer, etc. The first long trip I remember was to Adyar (near Madras), the headquarters of Dr. Annie Besant's Theosophical Society. She had visited Delhi and our school six months earlier. I was inspired by her personality and rhetoric. When Lalaji asked me if I would like to accompany him to Adyar where Dr. Annie Besant was holding a meeting of the Theosophical Society, I jumped at the idea. I had no difficulty in persuading my father to finance this trip. I enjoyed every single moment of my stay at Adyar and was overwhelmed with all the speeches I heard. I saw Krishnamurthy—a boy my age who had been declared an *Avatar* by Dr. Besant. I was, however, put off by all the adulation he was getting. I could see no special attributes in him that merited all the idolization. Later of course he became a savant, universally admired for his intellect, but certainly not as an *Avatar*.

Lalaji bought me my first camera on this trip and taught me photography. I still have the photographs I took of him at Hampi , Ajanta and Ellora, which we visited on our way back from Madras.

On one of the trips to Agra under Mr. Sarada Ukil, I sketched the Taj from the prison window of the Agra Fort. The imprisoned emperor Shah Jahan had gazed through this very window at the memorial he had built for his queen. Mr. Ukil was so pleased with my pencil sketch that he used to show it to all the important visitors who came to visit the school.

Lala Sultan Singh, first President of the School Trust passed away on June 3, 1930. My father took over as President of the Trust. He was an Honorary Magistrate and member of the Delhi Municipal Committee. As soon as it was formed, he also become a member of the New Delhi Municipal Committee. He left the management of the school curriculum and administration to Lala Raghubir Singh and Miss Kamala Bose, as Lala Sultan Singh had done. But he realized the importance of the school shifting to New Delhi and having its own building, Sobha Singh was closely connected with the planning and development of the building and got the administration to give the Modern School a twenty-five acre plot of land on Barakhamba Road. Most of the other Trustees were not favourably inclined to this proposal. All of them lived in the old city and saw no future in New Delhi. They argued that New Delhi would only consist of a few government officials and very few children to fill up the school. But Lala Sultan Singh backed Sobha Singh's proposal and the building and planning of the school was left to him.

Sobha Singh engaged Messrs. C.G. and F.B. Blomfield as architects. The Blomfield brothers were architects form England. Initially they had come on Lutyens' and Bakers' team of architects but later set up their own firm. The Blomfields designed the whole of Connaught Place, and their own offices were centrally located here in B Block on the first floor just above the Bata Shoe Company. Almost all the shops were planned by them, as well as the Imperial Hotel and a large number of residential New Delhi bungalows. They built their own residence at the junction of Janpath and Aurangzeb Road. In 1935 this house was bought by the founder of Pakistan Mr. M. A. Jinnah, and sold it to the Dalmias who made it into the All-India Cow Protection Society. In 1947 the government declared it evacuee property. Currently it is the residence of the Netherlands Ambassador.

The construction of the building was started by Sobha Singh with his own staff to supervise it. The progress was slow as the funds for the building were not coming in fast enough. He put in his own money and got donations from friends to finance the project. I used to drop in to see the building on my way to and from college. Unfortunately Lala Sultan Singh did not live to see this new school building.

In the crisp, early morning of January 4, 1933 the staff and students marched from the Daryaganj school to the new building on Barakhamba Road. It was a very touching moment as we sadly said goodbye to the old school but joyously set foot in the new premises. I had cut college to join in the march and participate in this important event. I felt so much a part of the school, both as one of the first students and also because of the family's close association with it. By this time the student population was about one hundred and fifty. Most other schools in Delhi had over eight hundred students but Modern School became the leading school in all spheres of education and sports. It therefore became the most sought after school with parents.

In 1935, the founder of the school, Lala Raghubir Singh, suffered a stroke. It was tragic to see this energetic and active man confined to a wheel chair. His willpower and devotion to the cause of the school enabled him to surmount this handicap. Confined to the wheel chair though he was, he came to the school regularly, right from the morning till the evening. Most of the daily work, however, had to be shouldered by the principal, Miss Kamala Bose. At this stage Sobha Singh also had to take on more responsibilities and became more deeply involved in the school's affairs. He ensured the school's high profile by inviting distinguished guests. The school was honoured by visits form leaders like Mahatma Gandhi, Pandit Jawaharlal Nehru, Babu Rajendra Prasad, Rabindranath Tagore, Rev. C.F. Andrews and Maulana Azad. One such occasion was captured in a photograph I took of Tagore with the school children and Sobha Singh in 1936.

All these responsibilities of administration of a rapidly growing school started telling on Miss Bose. The Trustees reluctantly had to look for a new principal to take over these complex and growing administrative responsibilities. Miss Bose had ably led the school for twenty-seven years. That would take its toll on any person. In 1947 the Trustees chose M.N. Kapur to succeed her as Principal. He was the youngest of the four of five applicants, and with no previous experience for the job. A teacher from Mayo College, Ajmer, he had done his M.Sc. from Government College, Lahore. His dynamism and youth impressed the Trustees and they were convinced that he would gain experience in due course under Lalaji's guidance. This decision of the Trustees proved correct. Under the able leadership of Principal M.N. Kapur the school went from strength to strength.

Mr. M.N. Kapur was principal of the school till 1977. The Trustees were forced to retire him as some ambitious teachers applied to the Education Directorate that the Trustees were not giving a chance to senior teachers by allowing Mr. Kapur extensions after the age of superannuation.

The growing demand for school admissions made the Trustees aware that another school was needed to cope with this requirement. As New Delhi was expanding southwards, Sobha Singh persuaded the N.D.M.C. to allot a plot of land to the school on Humayun Road. This school, designed by Messrs Kothari and Sons, was still under construction in 1959 when Lalaji passed away. In his memory, Sir Sobha Singh as President of the School Trust, proposed to name this building the Raghubir Singh Junior Modern School. Principal Kapur was in favour of making this into an exclusively girls' school. The Trustees turned down this suggestion as it contravened the basic co-educational principal of the school. The school building housed the Kindergarten and Junior schools, as a feeder institution to the school on Barakhamba Road. It was also felt that there was some merit in separating the juniors and seniors as they did not always mix well in all spheres of activities. This separation has worked to the advantage of the children. The Junior School was extremely fortunate in having Mrs. David as its principal. Her ready smile and greetings made her a friend to the students and staff alike. She guided school activities and struck a just balance between academic and cultural activities and sports. By this time I was back in Delhi after my construction work in Nagpur and Bhopal. I took on the job of supervising the construction and maintenance of all school projects. I was also appointed the Honorary Treasurer to look after school finances.

New Delhi was expanding fast and the demand for schools was still growing.

The rapidly developing areas were West End, Anand Lok, Chanakyapuri, Vasant Vihar, etc. Sobha Singh was able to persuade the authorities to allot yet another plot of land to the Modern School. As ex-President of the N.D.M.C and also President of the School Trust he was successful in co-ordinating this proposal. He appointed Mrs. Rosemary Sachdev (who was a parent and had designed the swimming pool complex at Barakhamba Road) to be the architect for this project. The construction of this building was given to Messrs Competent Construction Company of Shri Raj Chopra who had also built the swimming pool at Barakhamba Road. This school started functioning within six months of its conception. Mr. Ved Vyas who was Vice-Principal of the Modern School, Barakhamba Road, was appointed Principal of the Vasant Vihar School. Mr. K.J. Vari, also a teacher from Barakhamba Road Modern School, later succeeded Mr. Ved Vyas as Principal. In my capacity as chairman of this school I worked closely with both of them. The school has been indeed fortunate in having such devoted and hard working people who made it their mission to make this institution the best in India. This school too has grown beyond recognition and is now the jewel in the crown of the Modern School Trust. Continuing its close association, the Sir Sobha Singh Trust has placed funds at the disposal of the school for a swimming pool in his memory. This swimming pool complex is scheduled to be completed in 1995.

After fifty-five years as a Trustee and forty-five years as President, Sir Sobha Singh passed away in 1976. We owe the steady expansion of the school to his dedication and involvement. Additions like the Boarding House, Sir Shankar Lal Hall and the swimming pool complex, in the Barakhamba Road school, were added at his initiative. The 'Sir Sobha Singh Block' of class rooms were constructed in his memory. As chairman of the Sir Sobha Singh Charitable Trust which donated the funds, I felt this would be a living memorial to his commitment to the school.

I and my family donated fifty-five thousand rupees towards the construction of the squash courts in the school complex. Continuing the tradition of the family's deep involvement with the school, I personally looked after all the construction jobs, and the architects and contractors worked under my supervision.

General Virendra Singh took over as President of the School Trust in 1993. Under his dynamic leadership the school is celebrating its platinum year. He has set upon himself the daunting task of collecting ten to twelve crore rupees for executing important projects for the school.

When the school celebrates its centenary year in 2020, the present generation, who shared in Lala Raghubir Singh's dream, will not be participating. The buildings named after those associated with the school will be symbols of their dedication, but they will only be edifices if this present generation does not infuse the spirit of selfless dedication. Every Modernite is a testimony of that guiding spirit. I pray and hope that the power of Lalaji's ideals will continue to inspire many generations to come.

So Far And Yet So Near

Bharat Ram

I am one of the oldest students of the Modern School, whose age exceeds that of the School which is in its Platinum Jubilee year. When I recall my years at the school from 1924 to 1931, they are at once so far away and yet so near. My childhood is recreated in all its innocence and ignorance but imbued with a new meaning. Many scenes and images build up on the canvas and project a world which is totally different from what is now.

I can hear the trot of the horses, an occasional motor car horn and the chimes of the temple. Delhi's population then was around 4.5 lakhs as against 95 lakhs or more today. This staggering increase in numbers takes a toll on human values, besides placing pressure on infrastructural facilities, more so when these facilities have not been proportionately strengthened. The difference in milieu is both manifest and marked.

My mind's eye brings to the fore a leisurely Delhi. While the walled city was crowded, by no means the way it is now, the roads and streets were free from any kind of congestion. New Delhi had acres and acres of green, large roundabouts from which ran tree-lined avenues and a few bungalows. When my father built his house on Curzon Road, now Kasturba Gandhi Marg, it was a great adventure for us, youngsters, to see the progress of the work for we often lost our way, and it was even difficult to come across a passerby to ask for directions.

If I write about my childhood years, so distanced by time, it is mainly because of information gathered later. Even before I joined the Modern School, when I was hardly three or four years old, I was sent to a school called the Commercial School. This school was in Bazar Sita Ram in old Delhi, close to our home. It was started by my father after the First World War and it catered to the community in the vicinity. It was later when we were living in Civil Lines that I was admitted to the Modern School in Daryaganj. My father and uncle were instrumental in my joining the Modern School as they felt that Lala Raghubir Singh would build an institution where he will endeavour to combine Indian values with western progressiveness.

I do not remember if we were ever told why Modern School was established. It is only in the fulness of time that I have come to appreciate the ideas and ideals of the founder, Lala Raghubir Singh. He was a man of vision fired with a mission. He was purposive to the end, but, at the same time, highly resilient and remarkably sensitive to the higher planes of mind and thought. The central criterion of progress to him was self-reliance and he found the truth and power of the ideal in the practical.

Raghubir Singh desired that middle-class Indian youth be imparted instruction on the same, if not better lines, as in the public schools in England and in the prestigious select schools for sons of Indian princes set up by the British in India. In short, to provide the right stimulus to the indwelling spirit, the right ideas, including aggressiveness in the right place. According to Lala Raghubir Singh education should be such as to provide a system where the physical, mental and spiritual faculties may be given the fullest scope for development. It was assured and hoped that they would later shoulder civic responsibilities, coming as they did in the wake of changing political conditions.

Being a known personality of Delhi, Lala Raghubir Singh, was frequently visited by eminent men such as Mahatma Gandhi, Rabindranath Tagore, Hakim Ajmal Khan, C.F. Andrews and many others who were known for their liberal views, high values and sterling character. The guidance that I got from him and the school eventually made me what I am today. He succeeded in blending the best of both worlds, the ancient and the modern. Even in those primitive and backward days of India under the British rule, he went ahead to ensure that the Modern School was co-educational, and that its students belonged to all religious denominations. In the early years the student strength was also thin. When I left the school in 1931, there were hardly seventy students. So it was possible to combine *gurukul* and modern public school principles and teachings. Lala Raghubir Singh realised the need for a modern and open society in those days where boys and girls as students, and men and women as teachers would grow to become responsible citizens working alongside for promotion of a disciplined and ethical society. The combination of students and the teaching staff was from different religious faiths. We had at least half female teachers and girl students. I cannot help but wonder after so many years that the head of the school in my time was a lady, Miss K. Bose. In retrospect, I can only say that talent at no time succumbed to gender discrimination. The emphasis was on total development of students and on character building. Teachers evoked special values in us: they considered themselves privileged to serve as custodians of their young flock.

Lala Raghubir Singh also saw to it that day students were subjected to a residential regimen. They had to be in school from 7 a.m. to 7 p.m. Breakfast, lunch and tea were served, siesta was compulsory, and also participation in physical exercise and sport. Every one of us had to play games like hockey, football and cricket. If any body missed organised sports, he or she had to make rounds of the play-ground. The meals served were wholesome but spartan. For some reason of health, probably, brinjals and neem leaves were invariably on our menu. Even now, I cannot think of them without recalling the school days.

Not to be left out on fun and enjoyment, I remember musical programmes by eminent maestros. Playing Holi in Lala Raghubir Singh's house raises vivid memories of those days. It was not only gulal and chandan, but colours of all sorts that made the festival great fun. The entire school had its Holi Lunch with the Raghubir Singh family. While there were no formal and stereotype religious sermons, each day some teacher led the prayers reciting from the teachings of the Buddha, Christ, Mohammad and other great personages like Vivekananda, Aurobindo Ghosh and Tagore.

Individual attention was given to each student by the school management and the teacher. At the suggestion of Lala Raghubir Singh, I was held back for a year though I had been successful in passing every year. This was a wise decision. I obtained second rank in my final matriculation examination. While my grandfather wanted me to join business immediately after I finished school, Lala Raghubir Singh's advice prevailed upon him and I was sent to college for higher education so that I would understand business better. He was sure that in times to come, higher education would be to my benefit. I was so happy as that was also my wish.

So far as the curriculum was concerned, we went through the same paces as generations of students before and since, particularly in the arithmetic class. There were questions about the specific time when two trains running in opposite directions with different speeds would cross each other, and also the interest that would have to be paid on a loan over a period of time when a part of the Principal amount was periodically returned. This Iesson learnt much before the introduction of the decimal system, when the rupee was divided into sixteen annas, and each anna was composed of four quarter anna coins, or the length of a mile was eight furlongs, each furlong was 220 yards, and each yard three feet, and a foot twelve inches, has always stood me in good stead. My knowledge of the mystique of numbers earned recognition, as no less than a genius. Years later, in the London of pounds, shillings and pence, I could buy cigarettes and matches and hand over the exact amount or ask for the sum due to me as the shopkeeper was still fiddling with the buttons of the calculating machine. I have never been able to fathom why, even after the introduction of the decimal system , a sophisticated computer should be so much in vogue for ordinary calculations.

One of my unforgettable memories is that of one Rehana Tyabji who used to stay with Lala Raghubir Singh at Kashmiri Gate whenever she visited Delhi. She hailed from Hyderabad, and in spite of being a Muslim she was a great devotee of Lord Krishna. She used to sing beautiful Meera *bhajans*. Her melodious voice rang in my ears and I missed no opportunity to hear her sing, which she invariably did in the mornings. I would start earlier from the house to go to school and get down at Lala Raghubir Singh's house, which was on the way. I stood by the door of her room while she sang. She became a mystic and for many years stayed in Rajghat and died in Delhi. Even to this day her songs echo in my memory.

My school years, as indeed those later in St. Stephen's College, fourteen years in all, constitute a single memory. They do not easily separate themselves one from the other. Time for me, as boy and adolescent, did not 'pass' but it spread in all directions. My own happiness was perhaps due to the fact that I did not dwell too much on myself and made no distinction between myself and the world around me. There was a sort of heady well being, no doubt, induced by a fine appetite, good friends, lots of games, and a fair success in examinations.

How can I forget the chrysalis growth from short to long pants, the travel to school, on horseback along with my brother Charat, accompanied by a syce, and later to be driven in the first ever car purchased by my father with its bulb horn ? I cannot forget the down on my upper lip and the haste to handle a razor long before it was necessary, the embarrassment and excitement of fantasies about the female body and a host of physical and mental urges. Physical changes apart, there was the consciousness of gaining knowledge not only from books and teachers but from exchanges with people of different ages, classes and educational levels.

My college years brought a subtle change in my feelings towards my teachers. While in school, a teacher was a person who could do no wrong. College teachers and professors were a complex lot. By and large, we looked upon our preceptors as persons, not belonging to this or that nationality. Had I known, I would have echoed the sublime dictum of Newton that it was only by standing on the shoulders of giants that every generation climbs to new heights.

The effort to put together a substantial if not a complete collection of old memories is a joyous and also a rare experience in old age. A procession of vanished selves and of the selves of others cross the mind's eye. Were those selves not my own? It is generally considered that I am a very successful businessman and obviously my schooling had a good deal to do with it. All I can say is that my schooling contributed to my sense of values and Lala Raghubir Singh was the force behind my basic learning.

The School With Five Gates

Ved Vyas

It was the late summer of 1947, the fateful year. Along with my aged mother, three teenaged sisters and one younger brother, I left our home in Lahore, the cradle of my childhood, for an unknown destination in free India. After trekking, hitch-hiking, wading through neck-deep waters of swollen rivers and streams, travelling on rooftops of trains, we covered over four hundred kilometres to reach Delhi, the city of our future hopes.There were lakhs of people all over the city who were desperately in search of shelter and livelihood. None of us had any choice in selecting a place, even for temporary settlement. Destiny brought us to take shelter in two rooms of an outhouse of a sprawling bungalow on Keeling Road, now known as Tolstoy Marg, just two hundred yards from Modern School. Sitting in the courtyard of my new home, I could hear the loud and clear sound of the morning bell six days a week.

Almost a year passed in trying to find a job which could provide the basic needs for me and my dependent family. I worked at various jobs for whatever wages I could get, but hardly a day passed when I did not stroll along the boundary wall of the school and did not look through each of the five gates to see what was happening on the other side of the low wall. I could see the young gymnasts in and around the old gym building and the riders on horseback gallopping along the riding course. The hockey, cricket and football grounds were beautifully laid. In the manicured lawns, groups of students sat around with their teachers under the blue shade of jamun, banyan and moulseri trees.

I had never seen a school with five gates. My school in Lahore was respected for its academic results as well as sports and cultural activities but it had only one gate for all purposes and all seasons. My college had two gates. But I had never even dreamt of a school building which would be set in such an abundance of natural beauty. Twenty-five acres, just for three hundred students! The red brick building sat like a rose in harmony with the green expanse. It was filled with children from the lowest to the highest grades.

One day I watched a football match being played on the grounds. It was an inter-school competition. The school with five gates was playing with a neighbourhood school with no gates or even a boundary wall! There were more than a thousand spectators from the visiting school, lustily shouting, cheering, jeering and abusing. I went in and stood among the crowd. The Modern School boys were playing a technically superior and well-coordinated game but at no point in time were they even close to scoring a goal. The school lost by five goals. Somehow I felt sad. When I asked a boy why they lost his reply was, 'We play for the glory of sports and we don't mind losing or winning.'

Having played football for Punjab University in my college days, I instinctively knew what was wrong and why they lost. I was sorry for the young players because they had never experienced the thrill of victory. For me, while it was important that one should not despair if one loses, one should play to win, and win by fair means. What had cowed them down were the abuses and vulgar expletives of the crowd. Suddenly, I felt that the school needed me and I needed this big, beautiful school to give vent to my talent and experience in sports. The next day I walked into the school and met Mr.M.N.Kapur. Never in my life had I imagined that the principal of a school would be so young, handsome, dashing, warm and receptive. I had an image of a grim, weathered and worn-out face. The liking was mutual. He asked me whether I thought that the boys could ever enjoy the thrill of victory in the presence of hostile crowds? Yes, I said. They have to be trained to expunge fear from their hearts and minds. They have to be taught to become immune to jeers and jibes and learn to bear physical injury and pain. This attitude of resignation to loss had to be expunged from their bodies and minds.

I joined the school the next day. It was the month of January, the year 1949. I realised that the situation with the school was something like this. It had had, in its former Principal, a very competent, caring and possessive mother. What it had got in the person of Mr. Kapur was a father figure who could join the students in experiencing the joy of robust schooling. This was the best thing that could have happened because it meant a new approach. This also explained why we were losing in the common man's games. While we were good in elite, touch-me-not games like tennis, swimming and riding, we lost football and hockey. Our students could not score in a game which involved tackling and rubbing shoulders. The mother's role had ended and the father had to take over. My job was to uproot fear from the bodies and minds of our students. I did it by devising strategies such as heading the ball, tackling, letting the feet clash.

Partition had brought with it a spate of school-going children. Numbers grew at Modern School. Hunt was on for dynamic, maginative, talented and courageous teachers. I don't remember if we ever advertised positions. Educated young sportsmen, creative writers, talented performing artists were actively sought. I recall that even as a young man I had the audacity to dream of bringing great artists to the school. I went to Bombay to attract good people. Mr.Kapur shared this adventurous spirit of seeking excellence and aiming for the stars. Most of the teachers were hired first, then asked to do a B.Ed—first grab the talent and then complete the formalities.

During the interviews, Mr. Kapur used to say to the prospective candidate, 'You are a post graduate with a second class. I know you would be able to teach your subject better than a gold medallist. But what can you do with the children outside the classroom?' The selection depended on this aspect of the teacher's ability. Soon it became known in the teaching community that a good teacher with talent in any extra-curricular activity that could involve the children would be welcome in the school. A totally new breed of teachers from all over the country were ready to work far beyond their normal duties, along with the thoroughbred experienced 'warhorses' who were excellent in their respective subjects. It was a wonderful combination of experience, teaching technique, vigour and vitality. The school was gallopping ahead in all directions, the academic, the sports, the cultural and the creative. Within a span of ten years we earned the reputation of being one of the best in the country.

The Principal tolerated the idiosyncracies of the staff. They were unique individuals who could not fall into the conventional slots. They all had their quirks but they were honest about their work. Once I was rehearsing with a drama group near the art room. We were so engrossed that no one heard the bell. Mr. Kapur was a stickler for evening attendance. The next day came the stern enquiry from his office. I said simply that I could not hear anything when I was creatively engaged. He accepted my explanation. It is believed that the Lord Shiva used to walk with his *gana* (companions), the *bhalu*, the cheetah, and the *bhoot-prait*. What were these if not symbolic of different human temperaments? The greatness of Shivji was that he tolerated them all. Mr. Kapur too walked with his *gana* walking by his side like Shivji did.

There was freedom for the staff to experiment and innovate. Once a teacher had proven his ability and creativity he could give vent to his imagination and be sure of official support. Such an atmosphere and team work is essential for an extraordinary school. And it is with a sense of pride that I can say that we really were extraordinary in all aspects of a child's education. There were so many of us who ungrudgingly worked twice as hard to produce results without expecting any reward except the joy of working with freedom and in a team. Later, I was to learn that the management had given freedom to the Prncipal who, in turn, permitted us to operate freely. How grateful I feel to have been given this free rein to serve children all my life.

From a language teacher and a sports instructor, I switched over to writing, directing and producing plays and composing songs for different groups of students. In the course of doing theatre with kids we evolved a new medium of theatrical expression which I named *Rupak*. The narration of the theme was in blank verse which was interspersed with songs. The mime, action and acting was interwoven into a pattern. This was the nearest thing to total theatre. Themes related to India's independence, the country's endeavour towards progress, spirit of the national flag, national anthem and national integrity were put to this new theatrical form. Themes were selected to make the students aware of the importance of their heritage. These things were of seminal importance at that time. One of the songs in *Ek Lakshya Ek Abhiyan* had the following lines:

Kaan dey ke sun zara
Keh raha tiranga kya
Keh raha hai ye tujhe
Jab talak hain bhai tere nange bhuke mar rahe
Door unsey chand kadam sona chandi jhar rahe
Tab talak na mere neeche a ke koi geet ga
Keh raha hai ye tujhe.

Without any support or inspiration from governmental programmes and schemes, we were doing all the things which have today become the tedious responsibility of governments. In our presentations there were no theatrical sets, no costumes, no special light effects and no props. The students performed in the school uniform. It was very simple but the tight interweaving of music, mime, dramatic narration and action made it total theatre. It was informative, educative, elevating—most suitable for the schools which could not afford the high cost of theatre productions. I cannot forget the day when our Prime Minister Mrs.Indira Gandhi came to see the presentation of *Ek Lakshya Ek Abhiyan,* a forty-five minute musical saga about independence and the nation's march towards progress.

The school with five gates was really a workshop. It was an educational laboratory, where the winds carrying ideas, innovations, experimentation, and educational technology freely entered and reached out to the students. The students learnt effortlessly through their five senses. Proof of this total involvement was the fact that the students and teachers enjoyed every moment of the long hours, from sunrise to sunset. I left Modern School, Barakhamba Road, in 1975 to take over the headship of Modern, Vasant Vihar. Although I left behind the five gates and went to a school with only two gates, I took with me the essence of true learning—freely through the five human senses—which to my mind were represented by the five gates. I hope the five gates will always remain open and the students of the school will keep receiving through them all the wherewithal needed to meet the challenges of the twenty-first century.

The School As I Knew It

Madhusudan Panikkar

I spent nine years of my life in Modern School from 1929 to 1938, doing my matriculation at the age of sixteen. These were, in many ways, the formative years of my life but strange to say remembrance of things past comes in bits and pieces. I remember rather vividly, I do not know for what reason, playing in the sand after school hours in what was then the junior school, while waiting for the bus to take the hostel residents back to Daryaganj. Similarly about people. Some I remember distinctly; memory of others has faded with time and it is not the persons whom I knew particularly well that I remember most vividly.

Mine, I might say, was in many ways an exceptional case. Though I joined Modern School at the age of seven, my schooling until then had been rather peculiar. Till the age of six I had been to the village school owned and run by the family. I knew a little Malayalam and could do additions and subtractions. At the age of six, father took us to Jammu and Kashmir and a private tutor was engaged to teach us some English and Arithmetic. Thus when I joined school I was essentially a village boy with a smattering of English and no knowledge of Hindi. Moreover, as far as I can remember, I was the only South Indian boy in the hostel, if not in the school, at least in the early years. Yet the hostel was to become a second home.

Memories of the school in Daryaganj are extremely vague. The school on Barakhamba Road was under construction and the hostellers used to be taken by the school bus and brought back till the final move to the new building was made. At that time New Delhi, as we know it today, hardly existed. It was a vast area of empty space, even Connaught Place was only partly built. The school, therefore, appeared enormous and it dominated the area. During my years, the number of students was about a hundred. My own class, which was fairly large by the standard of those days, contained eight students. Some classes were even smaller. But by the late thirties the numbers in the junior classes had already started increasing. When the building came up on Barakhamba Road, it was the outcome of an act of faith, a belief that the future would justify. But to a young mind, it gave an impression of vast empty halls particularly on holidays when the school was empty of all but the hostellers.

What did the school mean to me? To be frank, I never thought about it seriously. It did and still does provide an excellent education in a congenial atmosphere and that is one reason why my children and my grandson too became Modernites. The school provides excellent formal education and the results over the years prove it. But there is more to it than that. The approach is holistic, it aims at the development of the total personality of the individual. I was not exactly enthusiastic about cleaning utensils or doing carpentry, but now I feel that it did serve a purpose. It instilled a feeling about the dignity of labour. I also used to wonder why I had to learn painting and music, subjects in which I had not the slightest interest. But now know that it helped some to discover their talent for these subjects.

Two things I must mention about the school, though I never thought about it when I was there. Surprising though it might seem now, there was hardly any communal or caste feeling. Nobody mentioned caste or community; there was no religious instruction of any kind. The emphasis was on ethics and morality. There was no regional feeling either. As I mentioned earlier, I was the only South Indian and, moreover, I was in the hostel. But even in the early days I never felt an outsider. The school was a community and the boarders formed a sub-community within it. I particularly remember Chand Prakash Gupta, who was five years my senior in school. When I entered the Allnutt Hostel as a fresher in St. Stephen's College, he made things easy for me.

During the years I spent there, the school was dominated by the personality of the Principal, Miss Kamala Bose. She was a formidable figure and both the students and teachers stood in awe of her. Lala Raghubir Singh, the founder of the school was always there, an avuncular figure, friendly and helpful as far as the students were concerned. I remember that we hostellers went to his home for Holi. He must have played a very important part in the administration of the school but I remember him mainly for the trips he organized, not only to places of historic interest in and near Delhi but also to Haridwar, Rishikesh and other important places.

One such trip I remember, rather vivdly, is mainly because we spent a lot of time playing cards on the train. The school took us to Ajanta, Ellora, Sanchi and other places of historical interest. Like most other school children, I was unaware of our rich cultural heritage; Taj, the Red Fort, the Rajput palaces and fortresses were familiar, but for most of us it was the first time that we glimpsed our ancient civilization. For me it was a moment of discovery.

In later years I had often wondered what exactly was the purpose of the education I had acquired in the Modern School. Its academic record from the beginning was impressive, but the emphasis, it appears to me with hindsight, was to create Indian gentlemen. An English public school perhaps served as a model. We had an English Housemaster who was in charge of the boarding house. There were other public schools in India but the vast majority of them tried to turn out brown Englishmen. At our school, the atmosphere and more important, the ethos, was purely Indian; it was nationalist in approach, although at the time, I was neither concerned with it nor aware of it. School was a place where one went to study and play.

I have a special reason to remember the school with a certain affection. As a child I did not keep good health. I had some minor ailment which required careful treatment. After my father had arranged for my treatment, it was the school which took the responsibility for sending me to the doctor every week. It was the school, again, which took me to a specialist for testing my eyes. I was admitted to the hospital for tonsilectomy, and while I was there, the Principal regularly came to visit me with grapes and other fruits. That kind of individual attention is not possible today; it was the small number of students in the boarding which made it possible. I even spent part of my holiday during one of my early school years with Lalaji and his family at Kasauli, if I remember correctly.

I will not say that the school years were the happiest of my life, they were carefree. The children are by no means innocent angels, they can be vicious and cruel and take pleasure in hurting. School life was not without pains, it was merely different. In old age when memories have become dim and one finds it difficult to recall names, events, and the link between them, one is apt to view the distant past with a certain nostalgia. Even taking that into consideration, memories of school days remain distinctly pleasant.

How The Girls Saw It

Ketaki Sood

One's memories of school days are always stronger during the last three or four years that one spends in school, the earlier years being a blur with only a few impressions standing out. It is the last few years which are responsible for creating an over-all impression in one's mind of whether one's school days were happy and memorable ones.

My earlier years were a blur of 'activities', not class room situations of learning the alphabet or learning to count, activities that included drawing and painting. My earliest reports state that I was happiest while drawing. I do remember that even though I had an older sister in school, I was not very happy leaving home to go to school. I also remember the singing of nursery rhymes with Mrs. Nelson at the piano.

As it was full day school or 'day-boarding', one hour was allocated for the afternoon nap on *chatais* or durees. But I don't remember actually sleeping. Perhaps, my mind was too busy with thoughts of the day's activities to relax completely and be able to sleep. No talking or whispering was allowed.

A little later, at Junior School, as it was then called, from Class III to VI, I was a little more aware of the academic aspects of school life. Perhaps it was because I wasn't particularly good at studies and found it a struggle to cope with memorizing 'tables' or trying to learn Hindi. For a year between the age of seven and eight I was in England with my family. Before that, we, that is, my sister, brother and I were in the Bengali section. The school gave the option of learning Urdu, Bengali or Hindi. After returning from England, we found that Hindi had become compulsory for all. Moreover, a year in England had set us back in most subjects, as the level of learning was much higher in India—particularly in maths. My memories of Junior School, therefore, were not very happy ones—having to struggle with several subjects. Also the teachers—Mr. Siddhu, Mr. Rajpal and others— were much sterner than the loving and caring teachers in the Primary School, then called Kindergarten or 'Babies.'

The only comic relief was provided by Miss Sheila Dhawan, who later married the well-known sculptor, Amar Nath Sehgal. He briefly taught art in the Modern

School. Miss Dhawan, who had recently joined the school after a stint in the U.S.A., found it strange that in a co-educational school, the boys and girls sat separately (the girls sitting in the front) and did not speak to each other. So, she decided to seat everyone alphabetically. We sat on benches, three to a bench. I found myself sandwiched between two boys, whose names also began with 'K'. But the result really was that the boys talked to each other across us, and the girls, since there were very few, became isolated!

Those were the days of 'direct current' or D.C. If a boy touched a girl accidently, the others shouted and laughed 'D.C. Current, D.C. Current' (*sic*) ! Any boy who was seen talking to a girl was teased mercilessly by the other boys. So much so that my brother refused to walk with me and my sister to school! He walked either yards ahead or yards behind, so as not to be teased by his class fellows! I do not know if it was Miss Dhawan's persistence or a natural process of growing, or changes in the atmosphere around us, but the D.C. phase came to an end by the time I was in the class VIII or IX. By that time there were school trips to hill stations and other places where boys or girls went together— accompanied by male or female teachers. There were committees and societies for specific activities in which boys and girls worked or 'sat' together, and there was a greater amount of participation by both sexes in things like House functions, ballets, musical performances, and the Annual Day functions.

Mr. Kapur, who became the Principal in 1947, also contributed towards this process of gender integration, mainly through organized activities as mentioned above. Earlier, the House system had one House—Tagore House—separately for girls. This was disbanded and the girls distributed in all the other Houses. Tagore House, too, became a co-ed House. Hobbies were open to all, and the earlier 'Girls Hobby Group' was abandoned. Though girls made up the bulk of the dance classes, the ballets presented at House functions and the Annual Day also had boys participating. The first teacher to insist on boys being part of the ballets and dance classes was Vinod Chopra, who picked some of the most athletic boys for the dance classes. They were reluctant at first, being very typically the 'macho' types, but were soon convinced that the type of dancing and exercises taught were indeed very masculine! In the plays, too, boys no longer acted in girls' roles.

Those years—the early to late fifties—saw a dramatic change in the relationship between the boys and the girls. It also saw a whole change in the attitude of the school and of the parents. Earlier, girls would study in the school in the lower classes and then be shifted by their parents to all-girls' schools. Most left the school by the time they were twelve years old. Though a few girls had passed out of the school earlier, my sister was the first girl to do the Higher Secondary from the Modern School in 1955, being the only girl in a class of about forty students. Two years later, in my class of forty nine students, there were six girls. Within a few years the girls constituted about twenty-five per cent of the total strength, and, for many years now they have been nearly fifty per cent of the total strength.

Were we a pampered lot? I really don't know. In some ways we were. We were allowed to go as a group to cheer our boys in an inter-school match, while only one class or section of boys would be allowed to go. When I was in Senior School out of a total strength of five hundred, there were only twenty-eight girls. Perhaps, the teachers— predominantly male in the Senior School—were a little lenient. But there were some disadvantages, too. We could never form a team of any sort to play in inter-school events. The only major area where we participated were athletics and here our girls were not found wanting. Three or four girls (from this group of twenty-eight) were able to find their way to State and even National level athletics. The only game or sport we were offered was basketball. We did, of course, play informally with the boys—football or hockey in classes VII and VIII, and cricket later. Other than P.T., dancing, swimming, horse-riding, athletics and basketball, there was nothing else that we could try our skills at. In P.T., Sardar Swaran Singh was as tough with us as with the boys. No wonder ours was the best marching group in comparison to girls of others schools—no swinging shoulders and bouncing steps!

In a way being girl students in those days, the transitional years, was good for us. We became very competitive, as we felt we had to compete with the boys and *prove* ourselves. We did not want to be pampered and be namby-pambies. We became tough, determined and ambitious. So much so that Mr. Kapur had begun (in his last ten years or so in the school) to warn parents of girls who wanted admission of their daughters in the school, of the kind of product to expect at the end of twelve or thirteen years in school. Particularly those parents of the conservative, business background were told that after the years in Modern, they shouldn't expect their daughters to get married at eighteen or twenty and be the typical 'homely', docile, 'Sati-Savitri' type. Most girls coming out of Modern opted for careers and professions or at least a higher education and a spell of independence in a job before 'settling down'. Many still pursue a career or profession after marriage and motherhood. Modern School made individuals of us, women who could think and behave and act confidently and independently, ready to fight for a cause and for their beliefs. To that independence and individuality we owe a lot to the Modern School and to Mr. Kapur.

As can be seen, my years in the senior school were spent in learning organizational skills through participation in various activities. Perhaps, I was a 'late bloomer' Or perhaps, as in most other cases, I came into my own after the age of thirteen. One's skills and talents become sharper by that age and one can put them to best use then—dancing, singing, sports or painting. My earlier interest in art (painting) was now noticed by the late Kanwal Krishna, who encouraged me to take the subject seriously. I entered several competitions—Shankar's International and On-the-Spot and won several prizes. I was also the first student of the school to take painting as a subject for the Higher Secondary. Though I am not a painter today, I am in an art-related profession and I owe it to the School and to Kanwal Krishna who recognized and nurtured this talent in me.

To the school must go the credit of selecting the best teachers in every sphere—in academics, in sports as well as in co-curricular disciplines such as painting, sculpture, photography, dance and music. The school believed that students would 'find' themselves and give their best if their skills and talents were allowed to blossom and flower; if they were given the opportunity of expressing themselves in other ways, that is, not merely through the examination system. Developing an all-round personality was a belief that was not merely given lip service, but put into action by providing the best opportunities.

Echoes

Shobha Deepak Singh

My years at Modern School are the most cherished of my childhood memories. The aesthetic, cerebral and emotional abandon of the students was synthesized into the shaping of a personality with distinct identity.My father was a Modernite; I became a Modernite and went on to marrying a Modernite; thus making us a truly Modernite family.

I consider my experience at the school as a special one. I had come from the Convent Of Jesus And Mary for completing the last two and a half years of my schooling. Looking back, I can say that this change was the best thing that happened in my life.The reason for the change was simple. My mother was keen that I should take up painting for my Senior Cambridge since I was considered to have some talent in the subject. The only subject I could have given up was scripture. The Irish nuns refused. There was a stalemate and the next thing I knew was that my school had been changed.From Shakespeare and Keats, I was suddenly deep in the throes of Tulsidas and Surdas. Nevertheless, the discipline and Anglicized mannerism of the Convent complemented the ethnic culture and values inculcated at the Modern School without the slightest interference of the one with the other. It is with this background that I look upon my experience as one that was exceptional.

When I joined the school, my first negative reaction was to look down upon the uniform that the girls wore. I wanted to retain the natty look without breach of the school parameters. I dwelt at length on how to sort out this rather simple but complicated issue.I decided to maintain the divided skirt look of the Convent Of Jesus And Mary by using the boys' trouser material for the skirt, and the frock material for the blouse. The combination was perfect and instantly drew a remark from Mr Kapur at the assembly on the first day that I wore my new attire.Other girls followed suit. At that time little did I know that it would one day become a permanent feature.

New to the school, one day I was attending the economics class of Mr Chaudhry. My long thick plait with ribbons was tied to my chair by some of the students. As I got up, the entire chair was lifted and the class had a good laugh at my expense.This experience broke me instantly into the student fraternity and what the school stood for. First a moment of embarrassment and then my joining in on the laugh—there was no look back. I value every moment that I spent in the school as also for the values that it engrained in us for all the times to come.

Being an introverted child, there was special confidence I gained by representing the school in swimming and performing for the Pratap House. The memories of participating with Amba Sanyal in the 'Kite dance' and 'Savitri Satyavan' under the direction of Narendra Sharma, forty years later, have stood the test of time. I can never forget the wonderful time in the arts department—the only one of its kind led by Kanwal Krishna and his wife Devayani. There was batik, charcoal for sketching, colours for painting, litho, lino, leather batik, and last but not the least, the potter's wheel. Along with these there were photography classes by O.P. Sharma. Mr Kapur's theme-based parties at his residence expanded our minds, and made us read outside the prescribed texts. All these laid the firm foundation of my future. These people became the exemplars for those of us who decided to let the seeds of our learning flower into a meaningful existence.Our destinies were being moulded and given colours and hues tapestry-like; and each student contributed to the fabric as he chose.

The trip to Ceylon(now Srilanka) for two hundred and nine rupees was another novel experience. We travelled to Madurai in fifty-two hours. Coming from a Convent , it was my first exposure to lilting film melodies as *suhana safar* and *hava mein udta jai* (with the girls' dupattas flying out discreetly to the boys' compartment)! We went to the Meenakshi Temple, and bought Madurai sarees . From there we were off to Kanya Kumari. Here we saw the awesome sunrise and then took the boat to Ceylon. We reached Colombo (I think there were 60 of us) and were put up at the Royal College for boys! The evening of entertainment of Kandian dance was too much for my exhausted nerves.After a good night's sleep we went out shopping.The availability of imported cosmetics was the girls' main attraction.We went on to Kandy and saw the site where David Lean shot scenes for his film 'Bridge On The River Kwai' and on to the historic Anuradhapuram.I recollect staying inside the train on several occasions , for several days. It is this intimacy, induced by force of circumstances that brought us closer . My personal relationships were made on this tour and endured for years to come—or at least till some of the girls got married and parted ways.

Each one of these incidents defined a distinct domain of our personality. Our positive characteristics were being carefully chiselled into our psyche. We were being meticulously honed for an unknown, yet well worked out future. Our character, ethical values and sensitivities were shaped not by chance but by design—and in my mind the person most responsible for it was Mr Kapur. We stayed the whole day at the school and as the gong sounded, telling us that it was time to go home, it was with despondency that I would get on to my bicycle and with Birindra Dhupia make my way home.

The spirit of gamesmanship and sportsmanship was inculcated into us at the school.Till today , I am proud of being the solitary female member of my family who takes a keen interest in matters relating to sports. I had been selected by the school for swimming at the Delhi Olympic Association. This representation proved to be my most painful yet memorable experience. Our swimming champion, the late Kiran Seth spent hours to make me adept in the art of spring-board diving and swimming. As I dived into the National Stadium pool for the 100-meters breast stroke, I heard the deafening sound of the cheer leaders of the school led by Kuldip Narang, urging me swim to win. I knew I had not made it. I walked into the green room and cried bitterly. Kiran Seth persuaded me to participate in the diving competition. Having composed myself , I dived off the spring-board. I knew from the claps that I had redeemed the lost honour and glory not only to myself but, more importantly, to the school.

There is yet another instance involving sports that I vividly recall.A group of students from our class decided to go to the Ferozeshah Kotla Grounds where a test match was being played . Chandu Borde, the cricketer , struck a double century. We came back to school and discovered that we had incurred the wrath of Mr Chaudhry for being late to the economics class. He demanded an answer to the economics of attending the match as opposed to coming to the class on time ! Promptly came a cheeky reply, 'Sir it is the application of the law of diminishing returns. The more we come to the class, the less we enjoy it'. This instantly earned the student a yellow card !

As the Founder's Day would approach, the whole school would be galvanized into frenzied activity and preparation. Papier maché models and calligraphy on chart paper(under the close supervision of Mr Sohan Lal Ahluwalia) was executed with utmost care.Every student's work was put on display. I recall Amjad Ali Khan's sarod recital for this occasion,Neera Kukreja's portrayal of Amrapali and Arun Shourie receiving school honours for his outstanding academic achievement.

Being asked to read a paper on Rana Pratap for the assembly, gave me confidence in the art of declamation. Each student's capabilities were tapped according to plan and areas of talent received a full opportunity to blossom.Thus, the mental faculties got optimum exposure. Simultaneously, our aptitudes were being tested to ensure that every Modernite would receive the direction most suitable for his natural propensity.

There was much that was expected and even more that I wished to fit into the school hours. There was Hindi tuition with Mr Vishnu Dutt, the basketball and swimming practice, the hours at the art department and the time with friends like Leela Shankar, daughter of the famous editor of *Shankar's Weekly*, and Asha

Randhawa, daughter of Dr. M.S. Randhawa, the expert in miniature paintings and horticulture.

It was this kind of stressed time management that has till today been a propelling force to make optimum utilization of the time at my disposal.Each of us had qualities that were unique. What the school did was to unravel hidden talents. These were harnessed for a future where each Modernite would leave behind not footprints , but create milestones.

Aspiration

Ashok Dhawan

1946. I was four years old. One fateful morning my father delivered me to Modern School on a tonga, and left, without once looking back. I cried my heart out. I ran after the tonga that was taking my father away. Someone forcibly picked me up and deposited me in the sand pit near the duck pond, outside the art room. I sat in the pit, crying throughout the day. I must have cried for a whole week, if not a month. The teachers were kind and sympathetic, but unmoved by my plight. The whole world had turned against me. It seemed only the ducks were on my side, clucking in shared grief. God, I hated school!

Kindergarten—what fun! especially the sleeping class! Every one was required to sleep for fifteen minutes, eyes closed, eyelids tightly shut, without a flutter—then wake up and narrate your dream! You had to have a dream, otherwise it was construed that you had not slept. When the eyes were closed, the imagination ran wild. I was flying into unknown territories—each more vibrant than the other. God—I never wanted to wake up!

Then came Junior School. The fun was over. I now had to study. I knew nothing. I did not want to learn anything. Maths was illogical, Hindi was a problem and I could not communicate in English. To express it in a word, I was just not interested in studies. All I wanted to do was play—go up and down the jungle jim, swing high up on the swing—that special one under the shahtoot tree! The teachers, unfortunately, had other ideas. I could play only during the sports period, provided, of course, I had done my homework.

On the playing field I would look in awe at those grown up boys of the Senior School, who majestically rode horses, imperiously led by Sardar Udham Singh. I envied those who played cricket, football, hockey and all the exotic games that I wanted to play! Then there was the P.T. and gymnastics instructor with an immaculate goatee and a very erect and disciplined manner—Sardar Swaran Singh. Could I possibly do all those somersaults? Was it possible to dive into the pool and not drown? I decided to grow up very quickly. So ended Junior School.

Now I was in Senior one, section C, roll number twenty. It suddenly occurred to me that I was a nobody, without talent and without any aptitude for studies. The established practice was to place the top twenty-five students, in order of merit, in Section A, the next twenty-five in section B and the bottom twenty-five in Section C. Roll number twenty meant that I was amongst the last six students in the whole class. All the teachers naturally favoured the bright lot in Section A. I was dejected. My ambition to excel in sports also remained a dream.

At about this time my world fell apart. My father died. We did not have the means to pay the school fees and therefore, it seemed I must leave school. I was too numb to react.

It was at this fateful juncture that Mr. Kapur stormed into my life, took control of it in a manner that only he was capable of, and propelled me towards achieving my life's ambition. I was summoned by him. The end had surely come. Legs shaking with fear, heart in my mouth, I entered the hallowed precincts of his room (the room that only a few privileged students could dare enter), and eyes downcast stood dejectedly near the door. A loving voice spoke, 'Son, you will henceforth receive a full scholarship to complete your education in this school. See that you are worthy of it. You may now go back to your class'.

Had I heard right or was it an illusion? How could one of the worst students in the school be worthy of a scholarship? But that is what Mr. Kapur was. His greatness lay not in granting me, and many others like me, scholarships, but in refusing to let circumstances destroy a child's future. He could not deny any child a right to education. His mission was to inspire his students to achieve the impossible, to look at life beyond the confines of the classroom, to ascend higher and higher and reach the realm of excellence—to become fine human beings! And to that end he dedicated his life. To him I owe my past, my present and my future.

Walking back to my class in a daze, the enormity of the situation slowly sank in. So far I had not been particularly fond of school. Suddenly came the realization that the school I 'wasn't fond of' was actually very fond of me! The sense of responsibility was staggering—someone had placed a load on my head by giving me the opportunity to continue. A feeling of fear crept over me. I looked around at a class full of brilliant students—Ajit Kishore, Arun Shourie, Suresh Malhotra, Ina Dhanda, Lalit Mohan, Sushil Choudhary....What was I? A ridiculously hopeless student.

It was a new beginning. A new life. I looked at my texts with different eyes. Until then I had been glancing, for the first time I started reading. I looked up at my teachers—so far I had been hearing, now I began listening. The classroom was no longer hostile territory where I would be made to stand in a corner, knees half bent, for not completing my maths homework. Nor was it a place where I would be slapped and have my ears pulled by the brighter girls as punishment for not knowing the principles of physics. Suddenly, I knew the answers. And I began to experience the joy of music, dance, theatre and the arts.

Mr. Radhey Mohan—'Chacha Ji'—taught me the fun and logic of maths, Mr. N.K. Bose, the art of communicating in English, Mr. S.D. Sharma, the purity of geometrical drawing that ultimately made me an architect. Mr. Ved Vyas exposed me to the passion and intensity of theatre which led me to the honour of receiving the school colours in dramatics for my performance in *Kamra Number Paanch*.

Sports was another world and Modern School its undisputed leader. Mr. Kapur, the sportsman, was never satisfied by the ordinary. In his quest for excellence he used to invite great sports personalities from all over the world to inspire us. The years 1955-1956 were memorable. I cannot forget the thrill and wonder of coming face to face with Jesse Owens, who had stunned the world in 1936 by his incredible feat of capturing four Olympic gold medals in one afternoon! Or Bob Mathias, World Decathlon champion, or Sammy Lee, the 1952 Olympic diving champion who was the first man in the world to execute the forward three-and-a-half somersaults dive! The Russian gymnastic team's visit to the school on March 8, 1956, left us all gaping with wonder at their incredible ability to perform amazing feats with the grace and perfection of ballet dancers. What dreams they all engendered in us!

The annual Sports Day was a carnival. It was an event joyously prepared for and was orchestrated with precision by Mr. Kapur. The athletes were stars—Deepak Narang, Ganesh Seth, Anup Kothari, Praful Jaitley, and many others. Then there was cricket, and I specially recall two outstanding cricketers—Vinod Dikshit and Bhupinder Kirpal. Bhupinder had a habit of gracefully leaving the ball—so we used to chorus, 'Well left Bhupi!'

Mr. Kapur used to pick up talent wherever he found it. Sham Lal was a prime example. The boy was a born gymnast, but had no means to train or go to a good school. Mr. Kapur gave him a full scholarship, and entrusted him to Sardar Swaran Singh. That was when a new friendship was forged between me and Shamlal. Together we would arrive at school at 5 A.M. Swaran Singh was waiting for us. I can still hear his crisp command on frosty mornings! 'Akhara khodo' (Dig the pit) and Sham and I got to work for hours on the parallel bars, horizontal bars, roman rings and all other apparatus. There was a lifelong bond created between the three of us. When Sardar Swaran Singh died Sham and I, his two 'sons', lifted his body on our shoulders—shoulders that got their power and muscle from his relentless coaching.

Modern School's intense rivalry in swimming with St. Columba's School was legendary. Mr. L.N. Khurana, our tirelessly brilliant coach, relentlessly chanelled our energies into a stream of victories. Wearing his trade mark, dark glasses, he would exhort his students to shatter existing records. New records were created in abundance by gracefully talented swimmers like Sushil Chowdhary, Ashok Jhalani and Parmeshwar Khanna. Our passionate cheering during swimming competitions at the National Sports Club of India '1—3—7—9 who does play fine—Modern School' and '2—4—6—8 whom do you appreciate Modern School' ! The hypnotic chants of 'Modern School'—'Modern School'—'Modern School' that rang in the air after our victory, the victorious team's visit to Bengali Market to celebrate with hot *jalebis*, the pride of stepping on to the victory stand to be congratulated by Mr. Kapur— were for me dreams which I longed to live. Could I possibly make it on the school team?

It was Sardar Swaran Singh, who made my dream come true. In the company of Sham Lal, whom he trained to represent India at the 1956 Melbourne Olympics, he fine tuned my rigid body into a marvel of flexibility. I could do all those somersaults I had dreamt about. I discovered, much to my amazement, the perfect equilibrium between mind and the body that has been properly disciplined under an able Guru. I made it to the School team and later the Delhi University and Delhi State teams.

Kiran Seth (Tippu) was the most graceful diver and undisputed champion of the School. One day I was at the swimming pool. Watching Tippu perform, I marvelled at his exquisite poise and perfect execution. He was like a bird in flight! Oh, to experience but a moment of such ecstasy! It must have been a loud, wishful, exclamation, for I heard derisive laughter. I turned to find a fellow student jeering at my stupidity—'Yeh moong aur masoor ki daal!' It hurt. Badly. He was right. I could not even swim. But to give up would be to discard all that the school had so lovingly taught. It was unthinkable.

Sardar Swaran Singh, once again, performed a miracle. I walked from the pool straight to him and said, 'I want to learn diving'. He was appalled to learn that I could not even swim. The next morning he took me to the pool and shouted 'jump'. I refused to jump at the deep end. In three days I was able to keep myself from drowning—just about. The next step was the diving board. Swaran Singh said, 'when you reach the bottom of the pool, push upwards and clutch the edge'. I did that. To this day my dear friend Anup Kothari is convinced that I did not know how to swim, and was only able to save myself from drowning by clutching the edge! Swimming was not my interest—I was a gymnast—all I wanted was to execute a graceful dive.

No one could beat Tippu's swan dive. So I did something that no one had ever tried before in Modern School—handstand dive. Before the week was over, I was executing nearly perfect handstand dives. I vividly remember the afternoon when I climbed up to the ten-metre diving board at the National Sports Club of India pool and did a handstand which caused a commotion. Until then, no one had attempted to dive from that height. I realized my folly the moment I looked down. There was no water in sight, only infinite space. This was suicide. I was too young to die. I must, very quickly, climb down the ladder and descend to safety. But that was not to be. The omnipresent Mr. Kapur materialized from nowhere and stood at the pool's edge. He looked up and transmitted wave after wave of his inner strength, infusing me with confidence, mitigating my fear and inspiring me to fly down with grace and dignity, to complete that I had started out to do. Those who watched me fly down from the board, said it was breathtaking. From there onwards was the victory stretch. Making the school team, winning the Delhi State Inter-School diving championship, leading the Delhi University and the Delhi State Aquatic teams, these were all honours for my school.

Could I have achieved anything without my Modern School?

The Enchanted Studio

Geeta Kapur

Kanwal Krishna had come to the Modern School wandering down from the Himalayas; he remained throughout a man of the mountains, painter of light. What great fortune that he was the first artist I knew. I was ten years old when he came to teach at the Modern School in 1953, and I suspect that I knew even at the time that he embodied a way of life that spelt what I would later call destiny. In Kanwal Krishna the sense of destiny was visible—so inalienably was his being resolved with his profession. Indeed at such a lofty peak of skepticism was his freedom perched that I could, even as a child, read this in the solitude of his gaze. When he died, at the age of eighty-three, the eyes were even more remote but there was still the hooded humour of his younger self. And he remained forever benign in the mocking spirit of a mountain mystic.

It sometimes takes half a life before one is ready to pay homage to a loved teacher, a virtual father figure in one's chosen vocation; half a life before professional rigidities soften and the barricades erected against possible sentimentality withdrawn. It takes so long to even find a style to pay homage, the style of speaking about one's formative impulses, speaking consciously about the unconscious. Now perhaps the pictorial motifs that have nurtured my imagination can be returned to art history where they properly belong, and memories can be returned to the gentler aspects of a period-history where they belong. In both these spaces Kanwal Krishna is for me permanently lodged

Heading the art department of the Modern School for close on twenty-five years, Kanwal Krishna made it into something of a preparatory art school. And it is not of course a coincidence that in the years after he joined so many students of the Modern School went on to art schools in India and abroad and became professional artists, architects, designers, photographers, art historians and critics.

That cavern of our fantasies, the art room, was all wrongly lit for it had few windows and no north light. It looked out on the crescent of the Kindergarten compound and you approached it, walking the path along the 10-foot tall hedge bordering the Principal's house. It was my daily fascination to see Kanwal Krishna walk that path at twilight with his slow mountain pace, his hands clasped behind his back. You could come to the art room from the front of the School as well, walking across the crackling red *bajri* between the building and the flowering gardens, taking a left from the compound of the great banyan tree. Or you entered it from inside the teaching block, through the dark and slippery corridors—past the class rooms of Mr. Ved Vyas, Mr. Awadh Kishore, Mr. S.P. Chaudhary—edging around the clay work paraphernalia presided over by Mawasi Ram (the Krishna's protege: a potter's son transformed into an artist and teacher) and then swiftly inside this aromatic haven of the art room.

The Krishnas, Kanwal and Devayani, inhabited that room like a lion and deer in extraordinary coexistence. The cavernous space was messy; it was scattered with easels and donkey seats and everything was encrusted with paint. Sheaves of the day's art work by children of successive classes lay stacked before a selection went up on the walls roughly tacked and easily replaced. In the ante room exuding the rich flavour of clays and dyes and wax, Devayani Krishna did her alchemical work with batik and ceramic. There was always this sense of happy production in the art room—and student work was often interspersed with Krishnas' own work, especially their prints that were hung up to dry around the etching press which stood in a corner, an object of great portent, as it signalled the skill of the 'master' that Kanwal Krishna had already become in the special graphics technique which he developed after his return from William Hayter's Atelier 17 in Paris, where he had spent some months in 1953.

This then was the art department to which were drawn not only art students within and beyond the hobby and class hours; it was also the place where the Delhi artists visited, making it into a proper artist's studio in the evening. Kanwal Krishna was a prominent member of the art scene in Delhi including the Delhi Shilpi Chakra. Among his artist friends and colleagues were Bhabesh Sanyal, Satish Gujral, Pran Nath Mago, Dhanraj Bhagat, K.S. Kulkarni. There was also the youthful critic, Richard Bartholomew, who taught English for a while in the Modern School and ran the school magazine, *Sandesh.* (He was my English teacher when I was about thirteen , a fact he could barely forget when I later became a critic myself!) Richard Bartholomew lived on campus with his striking wife, Rati, in a tiny apartment up in the red brick School building—adding, no doubt, his delicate, quizzical bohemianism to the atmosphere of the School and the art department in particular, where he made a life-long friendship with the Krishnas.

The Modern School then had this little subversive side built into the curriculum—it chipped at the solid middle-classness of its student population. I am referring to the Delhi business class from which the majority of children came in the first half of the School's life ; and children of the bureaucrats and professionals in the later period; the middle-class child being, one way or another, the staple product of Public School education. My father, as a Public School Principal, was conservative/progressive at once; what was unusual in the Indian context was his willingness to risk and change and risk again, picking the cue from the students themselves. He had acquired his love of freedom from three contrasting sources; as a student of the Government College, Lahore, which had produced virtually half of the North Indian intelligentsia including the rebel poets and writers of the Punjab; from the young princes he taught at the Mayo College, Ajmer, affectionately reforming their whimsicality into some form of Indian modernity; and from the youthful days in London as a student when he learnt to stand up to the British and test his anti-imperialist impulses. He was already inclined towards nationalism—in the wake of the Punjab martyrs, then for a period in an admiration of Gandhi, whose Basic Education programme he had keenly studied. Even as he joined the Modern School on the eve of Indian Independence, these impulses shaped into the unqualified Nehruvian mould. The Modern School was firmly placed in the liberal nationalism of Nehru in the decade of the 1950s.

To reinforce the consciously progressive aspect of the institution, he initiated an advanced fine arts curricula, and with the coming of Kanwal Krishna to the School, this intention acquired a further bold edge. Kanwal Krishna amused and tantalized him throughout. There he sat in the art room turned artist-studio in the evenings, brooding, imbibing spirits, pottering about in his art library that was our source of curiosity and education as well—Kanwal Krishna gave me my first glimpse of Van Gogh reproductions in that library of his—preparing and pulling out his rich, iconic prints of the monasteries of Ladakh and Tibet. Or standing with his hands on the little wicket gate of the studio as if it were the railing of a terrace house in the mountains looking out into the hollow night....Kanwal Krishna was the enigmatic, slightly wicked Lama to complement the sporting, open-hearted extrovert in my father.

The anarchy of the Krishnas' art room/studio was something to which my father took some time to reconcile; he always teased Kanwal Krishna asking if he would ever be able to get a relevant School document released from the mountainous piles of paper and art objects on his desk. He did reconcile to all this and more, given Kanwal Krishna's sheer stubbornness about routine School chores. He actually opposed these if they came in the way of his freedom as an artist while judiciously maintaining his dignity as a teacher. I have always felt that between my father and Kanwal Krishna, there was this most benign and good humoured struggle of equals to let the other perform his duty on his own terms; terms that were based not on some narrow notion of discipline but on a humanized plane of responsibility that included, had to include, a good deal of what I call anarchy that Kanwal Krishna held in his mystic mountain spirit. In turn, my father, in the spirit of a man who knew a great deal about the utopian possibilities in human nature, knew also how to hearken the call of freedom from the other spheres as the one to which his friend

Kanwal Krishna belonged.

All this institutional tug-of-war notwithstanding, it is hard to convey what a dream was nurtured in that art room for children who wanted to shed their tidy middle-classness. And if one should ever be lucky enough to visit the home of the Krishnas, a pokey labyrinth at the end of the School compound, well that was a visit with the good fairies in their underground hide-out. So many art treasures were ranged out in that house, and in Devayani Krishna's garden. And, of course children were not only allowed but invited to visit: that bewitched and bejewelled lady would in fact march a little band of children to the house to show them but one flower on a rare cactus as if it were some glimpse of a miniature moon. It should be mentioned that Devayani Krishna became over the years an immense influence in the School. A professional woman artist from a very early era, a travelling companion with her wandering husband: imagine the model she presented to the girl children in particular. She was a compulsive worker and in a constant state of wonder at what would be the most dysfunctional pursuits in life; modest and utterly individual, she was a virtual saint figure with green fingers who could make just anything grow. That was what her pedagogy was all about....

There was no strict method of teaching art in this art department—except that we were given the broadest brushes (after the vanguard manner of abstract expressionism) and encouraged to use gouache (poster paint) on large sheets. Or we were given the materials for painted batiks, for making clay pots and playful objects in the most advanced ceramic glazes. If one took art as a subject in the Higher Secondary course then the training was more systematic: I did some large life drawings from models on brown packing paper with the kind of rapidity and confidence that art schools may hesitate to allow; and I also did some painfully boring water colour still lives as part of the course. As for imaginative work, there was, besides the Krishnas, the Shankar's Children's Art Movement to boost our confidence.

With Shankar being almost a family member of the Modern School (all his children studied in the School; and he was a personal friend of my father and of the Krishnas), almost all the then famous On-the-Spot Shankar's Art Competitions were held in the School compound in which, I might add, the Modern School fared hugely well considering that there was such parity in the aims of the Krishnas and Shankar as far as children's art was concerned. Those two were among the most progressive colleagues in seeing child art as a spring—not only of creativity which is a well worn cliché in education, but of some historical sense of *contemporaneity*. If I try to explain this hunch it would go something like this: modern art, in privileging spontaneity has made a special place for child art. To paint in the manner of children is to open out the unconscious as it were, and from the opening out is elicited the preparatory as well as the most elusive forms of the imagination. Child art is a paradoxical touchstone for the sympathetic reception of modernity itself, of the modern spirit. Shankar, the shy, witty, and mischievous cartoonist (remember the famous *Shankar's Weekly* of the Nehru era) made a mission of child art, giving it a truly international dimension. His own vision had something to do with the support he received at the time from the national and international community—from Nehru himself who might have somewhere agreed that children's art was symbolic of the energy of an India emerging in and through its new generations and seeking universal affiliation with youthful forces everywhere in the world. Children's art as part of all round fine art education was a serious matter in itself and as part of a larger project for freeing the imagination of the young, for the Krishnas, as for Shankar in the Nehru years—before the harder forms of real politic took over education and culture.

It should be recorded of course that the Modern School, before Kanwal Krishna joined and even before my father joined as Principal, had an important pageant of artist teachers including the well-known Sarada Ukil and the great Ram Kinkar Baij who joined just after he finished his art school at Santiniketan. Though he returned not long after to join the Kala Bhavana Faculty back in Santiniketan, his legacy is shrined in the form of a huge wall relief of the goddess Saraswati in the entrance hall of the School building. Then came Sukumar Bose, protege of Asit Kumar Haldar and Biswanath Mukherjee of the same lineage. Here was the Bengal School as well as Santiniketan imported to this Delhi high school in full measure. This was a legacy that spelled a national style in art; it had gradually become, in fact, the official Indian style propagated in every major institution—even elite and westernized institutions like the Doon School had Sudhir Khastagir teach there for many years. In that respect Modern School up to the 1950s was following the canon of the national style befitting the nationalist framework which it had adopted from the start. It is interesting that even Kanwal Krishna, a man from the Punjab, had studied at the Calcutta art school, though following the other, more western, stream, he worked in a naturalistic idiom, producing these magically illuminated water-colours of Himalayan sites and its remote people. One way or another, Bengal dominated the art scene in the School as in the country at large—there were also other teachers with a Bengal education, M.R. Chaudhary, and Ritin Mazumdar, Sucheta Kripalani's brother and very much part of the progressive intelligentsia in Delhi after Independence. Then in 1952, under the new Principal, the appointment of Amarnath Sehgal created a little stir—what with his abstract sculptures lying about in the School compound intriguing students, bits of the moonscape dropped as if from up above, among the ashoka, avala and mulberry trees of the School's front garden. The very incomprehensibility of modern art that everyone is always amused by became part of the children's imagination. Then in 1953 Kanwal Krishna joined and we come round to the story I have tried to tell from the resource of my memory and gratitude... .

There were other artist teachers through the decades, overlapping with them and when they retired taking the place of the Krishnas. To name some of them: the well-known painter and enamelist Bishamber Khanna; the sculptors N.H. Kulkarni, Balkrishna Guru, and the volatile and sadly deceased, Ramesh Pateria; the Krishnas' daughter, Mridula Vichitra, and other younger artists.

Not quite an experimental school like Santiniketan or Dartington Hall were intended to be; nor the kind of eccentric education the dissident headmaster, A.S. Neill of England offered (though among the dozens of English Grammar and Public Schools my parents had visited, they singled out this odd school, regaling us with stories of the progressive freedoms in that famous set-up with amused admiration), the Modern School had at the best times its own eccentricities. And certainly the art room as the Krishnas created it provided one crucial cue. At the end what needs to be said about the art training in Modern School from the decade of the 1950s is that it confirmed some very basic emancipatory spirit of the School that was intensely nationalist and fully responsible but which was not fortunately prudish considering the number of risks taken in the appointment of faculty and the curricula. The test of much of this emancipatory spirit comes in the kind of girls the School held up as models. Girls who were always out there, in whatever struggle for personal and social independence the curriculum and the society opened out.

I wonder now, not being a parent, if there are some such cues left for the odd child to survive among the rich pack of parents and students—if such a child can survive and flourish as we once could, as a free spirit in pursuit of something so dysfunctional and splendid as art.

Learning to Feel Dance

Nilima Sheikh

The modernist nationalism of the experiment in education that grew within Modern School in the fifties and sixties specifically, is best exemplified in the role of the Kanwal Krishnas and Narendra Sharma. Principal M. N. Kapur's unorthodox initiative in seeking out practising modern artists to teach in school and providing them working conditions so that they were not too constrained by the exigencies of school education, paid dividends. By their own initiative, these artists remodelled the possibility of school education and revolutionised its scope. The philosophy of the school which allowed them both infrastructure and freedom, would have been conducive to the development of their vision. But undoubtedly it was their creativity, expressed by virtue of being who they were, their engagement, and the creative potential they elicited from young people, that reshaped the politics and priorities even of a progressive public school educational pattern.

Teaching children how to dance was not really the future that Narendra Sharma had visualised for himself in the early fifties. But the theatre world with which he had identified in the forties had dispersed, and his work in theatre dwindled. Married in 1952 to dancer Jayanti, he was choreographing dance for films for their livelihood. It was while on a tour to Delhi with a ballet production that he met M.N. Kapur who had come with Ved Vyas (already teaching in school), to see the performance at the Wavell Theatre near Imperial Hotel. The troupe was invited to lunch the next day at Modern School. M.N. Kapur had decided to persuade Narendra Sharma to join the school. What followed was one of the most fruitful interventions of the progressive lineage of modern dance born of the cultural nationalism of pre-independence India, and articulating the aspirations of the early days of Nehruvian nation-building into school education.

Narendra Sharma was born in a Brahmin family of lawyers at Aligarh. He had learnt about Uday Shankar as a young boy from his Bengali friends. Attracted by a photo graph of his in an Akashvani publication, he had secretly corresponded with Uday Shakar's newly opened centre in Almora. In 1939 he ran away from home to join the centre. Fourteen years old, shaven headed with a Brahmin *bodi*, a *jhola* on his shoulder and eight rupees in his 'half-pants' pocket, he arrived at this very modern, foreign-aided international centre at Almora. The American administrative director realised that the boy had run away without parental consent and so reported him to the police. He was allowed to spend one night on the premises but asked to leave in the morning. The boy left the centre but stayed on in Almora in a hotel, paying four annas for his room and four annas for food until he was spotted by someone. The police contacted his family and his maternal uncle who was young and progressive, agreed to support him. Thus the young Narendra Sharma entered the new world of dance, creativity and the performing skills. Modern concepts of movement, body culture and balletic form; a radicalisation of the function and scope of dance in modern times, the opening up of the great national resources of the classical and folk dance forms from all over India, and a search for a syncretic vision—for four formative years Narendra Sharma drank at this intellectually stimulating fountain.

After his training, for the experience of travel and for sustenance, Narendra Sharma entertained Indian soldiers. He was under contract to the impressario Haren Ghosh. They performed in Calcutta during the bombardment, then went wherever Indian soldiers were stationed with the Allied forces—all over the North-Western Provinces, up to Iran and Iraq, right into the war front of the Allied confrontation of Germany, spearheaded by Russia. After the war, the search for work brought him to Bombay. He joined IPTA, together, once again, with his Almora contemporaries, Sachin Shankar and Shantibardhan and *India Immortal* was performed in 1945. There was some disenchantment with IPTA and the Almora group of artistes moved away to realign as the Indian National Theatre. In 1947 they performed the *Discovery of India*. By the fifties there was a shift in the orientations of modern dance-drama. Pre-independence dance had been more creative and Narendra Sharma felt disillusioned by the revivalism that had set in. The absence of any emerging support structure heightened frustrations. The offer to work with school children struck a chord at the right time. In 1954, he joined Modern School and retired thirty-one years later in 1985. He left briefly in 1961, to work full time at the Bharatiya Kala Kendra, but returned in 1965 and eventually found a wider professional outlet through the Bhoomika Creative Dance Centre which he formed in 1972. A dance theatre for children was initiated in 1973. Bhoomika has maintained a regular professional dance company since 1979 and in 1988 a school of choreography was started. Bhoomika has a fully equipped studio-theatre for regular work and studio performances, with plans to promote a neighbourhood dance theatre in East Delhi. Modern School had been the laboratory and workshop for the language and form of Narendra Sharma's creativity and vocational passion.

The dance room in Modern School was up on the roof, behind the clock. When you climbed up those extra flight of steps from the reception area, past Junior School, you came to it —just after you noticed the sky opening up above you. Sounds of the *dholak* or *manjira*, or strains of music, if a performance was coming up, could be heard even before you got to the very top. The door was usually closed to contain the sounds. It was a wide room when you entered— twenty by thirty-five feet approximately, (if time has not falsified my sense of dimension) with yellow marble-chip flooring. A mural from the life of Buddha, probably painted by Sukumar Bose, faced you from the wall right across. A single wooden chair usually lay on your right, for Sharmaji to rest his foot for support if he was playing the *dholak*. Behind that was a wide range of musical instruments, some quite exotic, collected by Sharmaji from different places. Carefully covered and put away most of the time, they would be available in all their resonant grandeur when required. I believe the room was designed as a meditation hall. It is enshrined today in my girlhood memories as sublimated space.

We learnt to dance here, we also learnt to soar—aspiring, matching experience to the stuff of dreams, not with the perfect bodies of dancers but with our own gawky, forming bodies. 'Learn to enjoy and feel your dance,' had been the injunction, 'technical skills will follow'. And we did, whether they followed or not, but learning to express through our bodies seemed to become a possibility. It was precious privilege, I remind myself, garnered and claimed through the mass of inhibitions and restrictions placed by societal pressure and behavioural codes of class (middle or upper) and gender (cutting both ways) in the fifties. Even today the privilege abides as a psychological valve system, and, even more, a spiritual advantage. Consider, which parent sending their child to school would wager for a taste of sublimation on the curriculum? Our engagement with creativity brought us that—a spark contact with the artists' spiritual world.

It certainly brought us contact with the experiential world of the artist. Every year on Founder's Day there would be 'The Ballet' — choreographed and directed by Narendra Sharma, put together with help from Krishna Nair, his assistant, and Jayanti Sharma. Besides, for every House day there would be a smaller dance-drama or a folk dance. Increasingly, the motivated students were given more and more initiative in helping with the music, designing sets and costumes, shopping for accessories and in the actual choreography. Or we may improvise on a theme or idea just for the classroom, sometimes with access to costumes and musical instruments. I recall staying late after school hours, rehearsing for a production, the pre-performance tensions, music rising into the darkening evening sky across the roof, and the deep reverberations of the *nagada*.

The Founder's Day used to be celebrated in the open area by the old gym (where the new one is now built). A big open-air stage was erected every year with Mr.

Harprasad, our carpentry teacher, supervising its construction. It would grow in front of us, first the skeletal armature, reinforced and boarded up, and then, finally, dressed and festooned for the occasion. Stage rehearsal days were spent adrift in a stratosphere of collective excitement, leading upto the two evenings of performance in the chill of the early winter air and nervous exhilaration. *The Divine Cymbals*, a simple fairy-tale was the first ballet choreographed by Narendra Sharma at Modern School. *Toys and Tots* for younger children was often repeated on request—for Unesco delegates on one occasion. Improvised folk fables like *The Fisherman and his Wife* were, in the language of my *Sandesh* journalism of 1962, 'a thumping success'. *The Light of Asia* and *Meera*—dance-dramatisations of historical legends were followed by the even more ambitious adaptations of Tagore's plays. In *Muktadhara*, Narendra Sharma ventured to bring the complexities of mechanisation, development and dehumanisation to engage the mind of young people; metaphor in *Tasher Desh* was given performative extensions.

Take up choreography, Sharmaji would urge, since you like to paint and to dance—surely choreography is what you should be doing. But I took the safe way out, like many of my friends, and became a painter, perhaps simply because there were colleges where you could train in modern painting and after four or five years qualify as a painter. Whereas there did not seem to be any means to train in modern dance. Many years since, Narendra Sharma started his own dance company, and then his own dance school, singlemindedly pursuing the cause of modern dance, working in what often must have seemed a veritable vacuum. He remains even today committed to the ideals he started out with: progressive and secular, engaging through his art in the quests and frustrations of contemporary society and the existential angst of the individual, to a modern syncretic language and in locating 'tradition' to service the future constructively. Many of us since have learnt from him to carry these aspirations into our own work and lives.

Coming Into My Own

Amjad Ali Khan

Your son?

Yes Sir.

How old?

Twelve years.

Which school?

No Sir. He has been taught at home.

The man sitting at the desk looked up at his visitor. What he saw was a middle aged man wearing a large turban. Besides him was a boy, painfully shy, sitting at the edge of his chair. Both father and son had the same handsome features. They were in turn riveted by this man in an academic gown, with grey eyes, broad forehead, a voice which was simply electrifying. Three pairs of eyes held each other for a few moments. No word was spoken.

This was the first time I had seen Modern School. In fact I had never set foot in any school. Abba was afraid of sending me to school. He had one simple reason. 'His music will be spoilt'. Music was my life. Life—in more than one sense. I was born when my father was in his sixties, his youngest child. All his sons were trained in music but somehow it was I who somehow became responsible for carrying forward the musical *Virasat* (tradition). In some ways I became an old man even as a child. The days were filled with *riaz* and more *riaz*. During the evenings there were performances at which I was asked to play. I was an earning member of Abba's household at a very early age. School was a luxury I could only dream about.

In 1957, Abba left Gwalior and we came to live in Delhi.He was teaching in the Bharatiya Kala Kendra and we were given accomodation at the Ferozeshah Hutments. Our neighbours were Shambhu Maharaj, the senior Dagar brothers and Waheed Khan. Such memorable days! I used to cycle back and forth to school trying to beat my own record, threading the lanes and bylanes, flying from a world of art and artists to a world where boys learnt to become men.

For me it was a different world—this world of Modern School. A sweeping red brick building with pathways of red gravel skirting the verandahs and outlining the lawns . Leaving my cycle at the stand I used to enter the prayer hall thinking of my ancestral home in Gwalior, where the music room was also treated as a prayer hall. It was there that Pandit Bhimsen Joshi had come in 1938, having run away from his home in Poona and it was in the same music room that Abba had taught him *raga Puria* and *Marwah*.

My academic record was nothing to boast about. Mathematics was the toughest nut to crack. Mr. Menon used to look at me with his kind eyes and say, 'You who can make the most complicated mathematical calculations with a flick of your wrist on the sarod, what happens to you when you put your pen to paper?' The line that Abba and I always remembered was when, during an annual report session, my Maths results were under discussion. Abba looked unhappy and I was crestfallen as the marks glared at us from the register. It was then that Mr. Kapur spoke his famous words:

Amjad kabhi maths mein pas ho ga nahin aur hum fail karengey nahin

(Amjad will never pass maths and we will never fail him).

This was the spirit that Modern School infused into me which taught me to strive towards my goal.

On Making Up Ourselves: Theatre In The Modern School

Anuradha Kapur

I suppose the best schools seek to both 'school' the self, and to open it up—to give it a sense of potential, an understanding that there are many selves to discover and many directions that may be pursued. The means by which this sense of potential is developed is of course significant. In Modern School it was crucially through the extra-curricular activities built into the timetable.

It might perhaps not be wrong to describe our time at Modern School as an 'emancipatory education': an education that extended us out of the boundaries of the school and its textbooks to provide a powerful sense of the world beyond. For me Mr. Kapur's idea that the world in school had to be strongly supplemented with a world of theatre, painting, dance, and sport was exceptionally liberating. To my mind what lay behind this was a dream that Mr. Kapur had of releasing education from homework, textbooks and even hobbies.

In many instances school drama might be experienced primarily as a special show put on for spectators and slotted into the school working day as an extra curricular activity. But for many of us in Modern School, the extra-curricular activity formed the most important part of the timetable; not extra but essential. It was integral to the life spent in the school; and was the means by which we discovered many hidden layers of our being.

Drama in Modern School, what does it immediately bring to mind? Two kinds of experiences. One sort obtained by working with directors who came to help the students produce a performance; and the other fashioned by persons who were inspired by Mr. Kapur into making the school their home and teaching there. With them it was not just a show being put up but virtual options of self representation being staged.

Mr. Ved Vyas, Mrs. Sahay, and Mr. Sanger worked with the students at various times. They directed plays and took us through the nitty gritty of performance -- the lights, the make-up and the costume, the danger and the excitement of being on stage. The proverbial greasepaint and limelight thrill. But this was still a part of fun—time off as it were, an enclave of liminal experience that had little to do with real work, real life.

A moment, when the timetable stood on its head and this liminal time became truly a rite of passage into a world of art as *work*, also occurred. A memorable transformative moment. Which happened in the senior school while working with Mr. Ved Vyas. Sitting firmly within the timetable that Mr. Kapur had devised was space to learn and experiment with an extraordinary repertoire of songs. These were from the IPTA, one of the most celebrated modernist efforts of our cultural history. It was Mr.Ved Vyas who taught us these.

That these songs so reconfigured our imaginations returns to me more clearly now through filters of memory. The long and painstaking rehearsals, going over every word and detail and note and *tala*. The wonderful wooden floor of the old gym where you could tap your foot to Mr. Soni's harmonium with its strident keyboard work, the likes of which have now almost been lost; I know now that that sort of execution comes from the illustrious tradition of *peti* playing that made early modern theatre in India vibrant and evocative. IPTA appropriated it from the early cinema; today even its memories are fading.

It seems magical, even unbelievable now that songs became the vehicles of altering consciousness. But that is how it was. A sampling of the titles brings back a host of intense memories about the songs themselves but also about ourselves, about our bodies and our voices on which these songs were enacted. The songs were about peace, harmony, collective effort and *panchsheel*. I think of it as an unusual and imaginative move by Mr. Kapur to allow such space for the IPTA repertoire in the Modern School, where so many other public schools might have provided for hymns. For the songs mobilized us into thinking about a modern and secular India on the one hand and about an equitable world on the other, much as I imagine they mobilized listeners in other parts of India.

Songspace--a magic and active space in which we experienced a sense of the outside world, and realised we were connected to it; collective action, possibility of change, resistance, these words became part of our imaginings. Our place in modern India was 'real' and it was empowering.

These famous songs were later inserted into a form called the *rupak* which Mr.Ved Vyas devised. The *rupak* addressed itself to contemporary histories and social problems. A discursive form, it narrated the moments of the freedom struggle; or the story of the national flag, or repositioned Gandhi's words, Tilak's speeches, Nazrul's verses and Tagore's lines into our consciousness. In the process we, the speakers of these words, were situated firmly within the present of an India looking towards the future.

When theatre got linked with the world around us, then the very notion of school drama was refurbished in our heads. It changed from being a hobby and a diversion, to being a possible centre of our intellectual lives, a vocation.

Into this sort of moment came Om Shivpuri, Sudha Shivpuri, and Ram Gopal Bajaj, soon after they had trained at the National School of Drama.

The NSD of the '60s produced the best of modern Indian classics under the direction of E. Alkazi and assembled, as well, a stage vocabulary that was able to grapple with contemporary social issues. As an institution, the National School of Drama did much to make the theatre scene *modern.*

What, then, was modern in the theatre of the '60s? Chiefly, an exploration of the self—a mode by which the individual personality is explored, nuanced, and realized on the stage. The devices ventured were those that had been both debated and valorized by actors all over the world, how to *present* the self in the here and now, how to be 'real' and 'truthful' in performance, these were the canons that were put in place in the working methods of the NSD.

The dramatic text was opened up to the presence of the actors themselves; texts were not something you conformed to or even confirmed; they were something you created *through* yourselves, through the silences and the pauses that you yourself formulated. At the very heart of all this was of course something that is central to education, a querying of the self and its resources.

Although modern Indian theatre was on the upswing in the '60s, it was still scarcely possible for actors to earn a living only by theatre. Charismatic as they were on the stage, Om Shivpuri, Sudha Shivpuri, and Ram Gopal Bajaj needed jobs. So as part of his enlightened policy regarding the placement of artistes on the campus, Mr. Kapur offered the young graduates employment. He was sure that their presence would enrich his students at Modern School, while getting a regular salary would enable the actors themselves to pursue their lives in the theatre. For many of us, their being around and about us—I remember Om Shivpuri hurtling to class, chappals flying off his feet, a clutch of books in his hands, what were they, Hindi textbooks, grammar or that magical thing called a play?—awakened a passion for the theatre that has been lifelong.

Many memories of the Modern School of that time float to mind: in the old moldering pavilion, under the great banyan tree, in the classrooms even, all manner of rehearsals took place; Om Shivpuri enthralling the students by explaining the feel of the pause and of silence in a play; Sudha Shivpuri unravelling the magic of the spoken word to her students; Ram Gopal Bajaj telling a young actor how to be *real* while walking across the stage chewing on a *datun*; Om Shivpuri directing the plays of Dishantar in his small house on campus; every part of that house was crowded by young actors marking their scripts, learning their lines and dreaming up characters in the texts. All this while the Modern School precinct was dotted with Delhi's amateur groups rehearsing their plays wherever space was found. Not one but many artistes in residence!

A small anecdote. It is a matter of pride for us from the Modern School, that one of the classics of modern Indian theatre, *Adhe Adhure* was rehearsed by Om Shivpuri at the Modern School for many, many months. The set was almost completely built inside the damp pavilion of the football field. Every word was closely analysed, motivations debated and then underscored, and a light and shadow etched onto contemporary middle-class people, individuals, identities. During the long rehearsal period Mohan Rakesh, the author of *Adhe Adhure* was also there, cigar in hand, looking unflinchingly through his glasses at every move, twitch, *gesture*, that the actor performed and commenting on any wayward pronunciation that might occur.

In some senses this was a sign of the vital and generous atmosphere that the school had at that time.

Om Shivpuri jostled his students into reworking the great classics upon themselves; Lear or the Fool or Antigone, their emotions had to be staged; that was the scale of the space that had to be inhabited and fashioned by student actors. Maya Rao, today a distinguished actor-dancer, remembers the way the storm tumbled out of the mouth of a young actor when Shivpuri sat on his back and pounded him, the better to remind him of Lear's enormous grief, his abandonment and bewilderment. She remembers too how the world of the Fool was carved by her after Om Shivpuri provided her with clues, openings, questions; how the sound of the storm entered her heart through her ears and uplifted her into a realm of fantasy and possibility where the muddy gunnysack he had asked her to cut holes in for her costume became the very texture and life of the Fool's rough hewn words. The universes of these great characters were made up through the pushes,the provocations and the buffetings that Om Shivpuri delivered to us. These made us discover persons within ourselves that could invent other identities. The adventure of thinking up yourself in the world of texts was heady, it was the stuff of dreams.

Another memory comes to mind. Richard Schechner, a distinguished director from the USA, came to Delhi with the Performance Group and his version of Brecht's *Mother Courage*. I remember it to be one of the finest productions of the play that I have ever seen. The performance was mounted in the school gym where scaffolding, ropes and lights were set up to make an environmental set. The version performed was magnificent, unsettling and far from palatable. Sequences depicting violence in the wake of war were tough, and perturbed the middle-class audiences. Censor the scenes? No, said Mr.Kapur, we'll stand by them as they are integral to the view of the play and are not there for titillation. For us it was a lesson about commitment to work, and to the artist's freedom to invent, create, disturb, to make us think.

This sort of education made us consider intellectual choices that were, and perhaps still are, rare in most public schools. Aspirations of making a career as theatre practitioners, dancers, painters, writers were not uncommon in the Modern School of our time.

It was because of Mr.M.N.Kapur's vision that some of the most charismatic performers of the modern Indian stage were persuaded to come to Modern School. As a result, we could dream of a life in art. In a sense, it is surprising that a public school has produced so many kinds of artists. But in another sense, it is not surprising at all. For built into the school was place to desire alternate visions and idealistic lives.

What India Means To Me

Anwar Abbas

An institution is the lengthened shadow of one man.

— Ralph Waldo Emerson

The year was 1970. The month was August when most of India is sizzling hot. After the twenty-five-odd *baraatis* travelling by train from Bombay to Karachi via Delhi, Amritsar, Wagah and Lahore had been comfortably seated in the three-tier second class compartment, I took a sigh of relief. Even as the most important member of the team, the bridegroom, I was required to make most of the arrangements for the journey and to see that everyone in the party, including my friend Ghanshyam Rohera, who was visiting his ancestral home in Sindh for the first time in his life, were comfortable in every way. The training, never to shy away from any responsibility however small or however onerous, had been grilled into me by Uma Shankar Nigam, Subhash Housemaster who had handpicked me even as a 'junior' in the Senior School when the number of Houses expanded from eight to twelve in 1957.

As I extracted the handkerchief to wipe the sweat from by brow, out fell the printed post-card neatly signed by our Sanskrit teacher, Dr. K. D. Bhardwaj reminding me 'for the last time' to rush my contribution for the Golden Jubilee Number of the Modern School which 'is already in the press.' In all the din and excitement of getting married I had all but forgotten my promise. I jumped out of the train, bought the first note-book and a pencil I could lay my hands on at the A.H. Wheeler stall and, on returning to the compartment and my window seat, I began writing the heading of the article, 'My Own Golden Jubilee.' For the next couple of hours everything around me just did not exist. The first draft was ready for being mailed from Delhi when the train steamed into Ratlam.

In April 1995, at seven in the morning, I receive a long distance call from my cousin, Syeda, from Delhi. 'We are bringing out a special on the occasion of Modern School's Platinum Jubilee,' Syeda all but shouted over a disturbed connection from across the MacMahon line—which has always made me wonder, both while in India and now in Pakistan, whether the disturbance is technical or political in nature. 'Your contribution for the book, which will be edited by Mr. Khushwant Singh and I, is a must. So get to your computer and start right away.'

Only the day earlier, I had told two of my colleagues, Iqbal Ahmed, the Principal, and Muslim Habib, the Trustee of the School in Karachi of which I am now the Administrator, that I am getting a bit tired of their ramblings about 'the old days', the old students, retired teachers, and former Principals. Would they please get on with the agenda of the meeting and permit me to leave before they carry on about their old-boy ties! Muslim Habib is also an old student and Iqbal has been associated with the school for thirty years first as a teacher and now as its Principal. The call from Delhi had me all keyed up about my alma mater's 75th anniversary leaving me wondering whether it is really boredom with my colleagues' reminiscences or jealousy over my own physical distance from the excitement of being an active Modernite not too long ago?

The call from Delhi also reminded me all too suddenly that I too have, personally, covered a milestone. If Modern School is 75, then my wife and I have completed twenty-five years of marriage and companionship. No ordinary marriage this since the 'girl' was from Pakistan and the 'boy' was from India which left a number of people, including the Indian consulate staff who hosted a reception in our honour in August 1970, dumb-struck because it has usually been the other way round in the Indo-Pak 'matrimonial alliances'.

Back to 1970 and to the *baraat* seated in the train. We steam from Bombay onto the New Delhi station. All the visas for Pakistan have been obtained, except mine, because I do not have an endorsement for Pakistan on my passport.

'But,' I protest, 'I have an endorsement—for *All countries of the World*—and I would assume Pakistan is part of this world'. But such logic does not hold good where government rules and diplomatic relations are concerned. My friend, and a former President of Modern School Old Students' Association (MSOSA), the late Vinod Dixit told me many years later when he was Joint Secretary in the Ministry of Finance, 'Look here, Anwar, all governments have set rules and the grooves in which these rules permeate. It is for the people to adjust their appeals and proposals into these grooves, and not vice versa.'

To this day I am asked, both in India and in Pakistan, by friends and non-friends (agency personnel who 'interview' me outside the now-closed Indian Consulate at Karachi), out of curiosity, not unmixed with amazement, as to why I chose to migrate to Pakistan at the 'ripe old age' of forty-two! I had done nothing particularly wrong, I was not evading political or religious persecution and had not, to the best of everyone's knowledge, committed a crime or a financial blunder which had brought ruin! I had a fairly decent job and a satisfying, if not a glorious, working life behind me. I had a large group of friends both in Delhi and in Bombay, particularly, on account of my association with Delhi's finest school and the best-known college; with their large network of old students I had nothing to worry about, professionally or personally. Ever.

I bow my head, but not in shame or remorsefulness. I bow my head in gratitude to Almighty Allah that He gave me the rare privilege of being associated with such loving, affectionate and kind people, who gave me the opportunity for good education not available to a multitude of people in India, or in Pakistan for that matter. And then I raise my head in defiance to ask them, 'Would they have expressed such surprise if I had chosen to live in Saudi Arabia or one of the Gulf states to amass untold wealth, until my hair, (if any of it was left on the pate) had turned grey and my eyes cataract-ridden, never to have been able to enjoy the fruits of my labour of a life-time?' So what is the big deal about going over to Pakistan?

Do immigrant Indians stop loving India and its people, merely because they now sing 'Long Live the Queen' or the 'Star and stripes' anthem? So why should I? Merely because a handful of politicians on either side of the border wish it so? To me, as to India's professor-philosopher, the late Dr. Syed Abid Husain, 'India's (cultural) history of several thousand years shows that the subtle but strong thread of unity which runs through the infinite multiplicity of her life, was not woven by the pressure of power groups but the vision of seers, the vigil of saints, the speculation of philosophers, and the imagination of poets and artists.....' A heritage which is equally and proudly shared by that part of the continent we know as Pakistan.

My world view of humanity transcends man-made borders. My favourite Principal Mr. M. N. Kapur, never tired of saying how much he was indebted to his education at the Government College, Lahore, and how much he enjoyed playing hockey with the great Colonel Dara who moved to Pakistan after partition and after having served Subhash Chandra Bose's secular Indian National Army. Separation by borders and barriers never came in the way of Mr. Kapur's affection for Iftikhar Dara, so why should it come in the way of his pupil on whom he showered so much affection all through his years at the Modern School?

To understand fully what I have stated here, a Modernite has merely to recall the morning assembly at which he sang the words of Tagore and Kabir, Iqbal and Surdas and so many other harbingers of love, compassion and brotherhood. Yellowing with age, I still keep my Modernite friend Anand Singh Bawa's first letter to me written from the Indian Institute of Technology, Madras which stated, 'Anwar, people here attach more importance to things about which we never gave a thought in school.' Bawa was obviously referring to the rampant caste system in the South which he found abhorrent.

When my dearest friend Maheshwar Dayal died, less than a year after my shifting to Pakistan, I wrote an emotional obituary on him titled, '*Mard-e-Momin* Mahesh.' A number of fanatics around me criticised me for calling a Hindu, a *Mard-*

e-Momin. Why not? said I. If Mahesh complied with all of Iqbal's standards of a *Momin* then he can surely be called by that name. Indeed all of us are born to surrender ourselves completely before the will of the Almighty, and the names we receive are all accidents of birth and an identity of the 'tribes' to which we belong or are born into.

It is perhaps a coincidence that after spending twenty years of my working life with an airline and travel business I am now vested with the task of looking after the affairs of a school in Karachi which is not dissimilar to the Modern School in New Delhi. As we work to provide a good and meaningful education to pupils, I find inspiration from the systems and programmes of Modern School as I experienced it over thirty-five years ago. For me India will always remain a friendly neighbour with great commonality and the country where my school continues to march ahead towards it centurian year, whether or not I am around to witness the great event. Survival and progress in all conditions: that is what good institutions are all about.

Ashiana

Pavan Ahluwalia

If you can fill the unforgiving minute
With sixty seconds' worth of distance run,
Yours is the Earth and everything that's in it,
And–which is more—you'll be a Man, my son!

A day in Modern School is a long and hectic affair, each minute being 'sixty seconds worth of distance run'. Barely a few hours after the last IIT aspirant in the Golden Jubilee Hostel shuts his books, the first few football players are in the field for morning practice.

Modern School is, in a sense, a bundle of contradictions. It is a member of the Indian Public Schools Conference (IPSC), an organisation of fifty leading schools all over the country, most of which are residential. Given the range of extra-curricular activities available to the students, the emphasis on all-round education and development of character, as well as the fact that most students stay back in school until the evening on some pretext or the other during a significant part of the academic year, one would think that Modern is closer to its peers in the IPSC than to the day schools in Delhi.

It is labelled an 'elite' school yet accepts more students on scholarship than almost any other school in Delhi. While going through a list of Modern School parents one would find industrialists, bankers and Cabinet Ministers as well as bus conductors, domestics and typists. Once a student enters the school, however, social and economic identity are submerged in the Modern School identity. I myself was not aware that some of my classmates were on scholarship till we reached Class XII.

In its functioning and approach to education Modern is a westernised school. However, all important occasions in the school are marked by a small prayer performed on stage. The students sit cross-legged on durrees during assembly and remove their shoes before going on stage. Modern is one of the few schools whose rock guitarists are as accomplished as its sitar players. It staged the legendary Rock classic *Jesus Christ Superstar* on the one hand, and was the first school in India to have a SPICMACAY chapter, on the other. It is these various aspects that make a Modern School day the unique experience that it is.

The day generally begins around 6.30 a.m. which is when the school team members arrive for sports practice and are joined by the students of the Boarding House. At about a quarter to eight the school buses start bringing in the day scholars and the bulk of the teaching staff. Greetings and gossip are exchanged amongst the senior students till about a quarter past eight when certain teachers start yelling at the Prefects, who start yelling at the students, who are busy yelling at each other. The net result of all this yelling is that the Prefects have sore throats and everyone rushes to the House Meetings.

The school is divided into fifteen Houses: Akbar, Ashoka, Azad, Gandhi, Lajpat, Laxmibai, Nehru, Patel, Pratap, Ranjit, Shastri, Shivaji, Subhash, Tagore and Tilak. The Houses compete with each other in a number of sports and the best House is awarded a shield on the Sports Day. An Academics shield is awarded, on the Founder's Day, to the House with the highest average percentage of marks. The Houses compete against each other in debates, quizzes, dumb charades and skit competitions every Friday in the activity period. Every week a House is on duty, which means that its members wait on the Principal and Headmaster, deliver the news and the talk and stay on duty at the gate to write down the names of the latecomers.

The biggest and most enjoyable House events of all are the biennial House Functions. Weeks of preparation and fund raising go into these nights of dance, music and drama, put up by the members of the House for the faculty and parents. The House system in Modern, thus, plays a role similar to the one it plays in boarding schools. It enables students of various classes to work together, have fun together and learn to win and lose together. One learns how to respect and co-operate with one's seniors, how to guide one's juniors and how to work with one's Housemaster. Unlike in other schools where Houses exist in name only, in Modern they are active, functioning institutions that are the hub of extra-curricular activity in the school.

After the House Meeting, in which House affairs are discussed, some of the students leave for Socially Useful Productive Work (SUPW) and rehearsals of school functions while the rest attend assembly. The assembly begins with a prayer followed by a moment's silence. After the prayer a member of the House on duty reads out the news while another delivers a talk on the subject of his choice. These topics range from 'Why people shake hands when they meet' to 'The dangers of a unipolar world in the post-Gulf War scenario.' However after September it seems as though every speaker is a sentimental S-7 student and the topic is invariably 'My Feelings on Leaving Modern'.

The seniors who go for SUPW are divided into a number of groups. A certain kind of person is fond of labelling Modern as a haven for 'rich, spoilt and pampered brats'. It is these 'brats' who spend an hour or so every morning tutoring the children of the Class IV employees, weeding the lawns and cleaning and dusting the classrooms. There are, however, a few rather enterprising but not as conscientious souls who manage to bunk this activity by hiding in the innumerable nooks and corners of the twenty-five acre campus. One such offender managed to bunk SUPW for the whole of his Class XI and consequently had no idea what options were available. He was caught at the beginning of his Class XII by a teacher and upon being asked what his SUPW activity was, looked over his shoulder, saw some students weeding the lawn and replied, 'Ma'am, Agriculture.'

Three classes are held between the assembly period and the recess. If there is one characteristic feature of a Modern School classroom it is the freedom that is given to students and teachers alike. As long as the courses are covered by the end of term and the students are happy, the teachers can teach at their own pace, hold their classes wherever they like (the front lawn being a highly sought after venue in the winters) and undertake any exercise with the class without interference by the Heads of Departments.

The students are given a great degree of flexibility. They may miss classes for inter-school matches, debates, quizzes and even intra-school rehearsals or House work. The teachers help them out later to make sure they do not lose out on anything being taught in class. Part of the reason why teachers respect the extra curricular commitments of the students is that they themselves are accomplished in areas other than the subjects they teach in school. The faculty includes musicians, debators, actors, directors, choreographers, cricketers, badminton players, table tennis players and even computer enthusiasts.

Once a week, for the XI and the XII separately, the period before the break is the Principal's Period, where the students of the batch interact with the Principal in the absence of the staff members. In 'PP', as the students call it, one can get up and discuss or ask questions on anything one wishes to, be it school policy, rules, the conduct of a student, staff member or that of the Principal himself.

The recess, from 10.50 to 11.25, for the seniors and 11.25 to 12.00 for the juniors is when the bulk of the socialising in school takes place. The students filter into their favourite hangouts to gossip while the teachers retire to the staff room to do likewise. Six different football matches are played on the same field with eight teams and five footballs. Two kinds of people find their way to the canteen. The first kind are those who have something to celebrate. The second and vastly more numerous group consists of those who wait outside the canteen to prey upon members of the first. If any students of the school ever feel depressed about not having enough friends, the wisest course they could take would be to approach the canteen waving their wallets. In a few moments they would discover that they have enough friends to run for Parliament.

No account of the recess would be complete without mentioning the occasional 'Fights' that take place. There are two main types of fights, those between the Class XI and Class XII and those between the boarders and day scholars. The provocation is invariably the fact that a member of one group has picked on a member of the other. One side gathers near the canteen and the other near the football field or basketball court and each taunts the other. The Prefects line up on the side praying for a chance to use their authority. On the rare occasions that the two sides do charge at each other they never get beyond the first few punches as they are promptly separated by the school Prefects who make the most of this rare opportunity to emerge as the heroes of the day. The offenders are then dragged off to be punished in opposite directions, and the few unlucky ones with broken noses and aching shins are packed off to the sanatorium. In a few moments, the 'canteen scene' is as calm as ever and the only reminders of the earlier violence are the faint cries of 'Dekh lenge' coming from opposite directions.

Classes resume at 11.25 a.m. after the recess and some of the stories that are told to explain late entry into the classroom would put Enid Blyton to shame. 'Ma'am I was on my way to class but I was called by ...and given a message to give to ... who asked me to forward it to... who asked me to get her a cup of tea without sugar and as I was going to get it ... called me' (omission of punctuation marks being intentional), is one example. The more imaginative ones come up with excuses like 'Sir I was on my way to class when a genie popped out of the Campa Cola bottle with which I'd tried to break that cheeky S-6 er's head. He took me away to a far off land where I was married to an Arabian Princess. Then I remembered how you had always said one should serve one's country instead of settling abroad, so I divorced her, booked my return ticket and here I am'.

School is officially over at 1.45 p.m. Goodbyes, last messages, reminders, etc. are exchanged amongst teachers and students as the buses leave the campus. At 2.15 p.m. the boarders assemble in the mess for lunch, along with the students who are staying back. Though the boarding house students are perpetually complaining about the food they are served, I find it quite wholesome and reasonably tasty. After lunch the boarders go to their rooms to study or to the field for sports practice. The day scholars go for whatever practice they were staying back to attend. Bengali Market is overflowing with students in the easily identifiable blue uniform. Nathu's, Bengal Sweets and New Janata Book Depot owe a significant chunk of their clientele to the school. In fact the owners of some of these shops have sent their children to Modern. Until about 5 p.m. it is not uncommon to step into the school and find a couple of hundred students, excluding the boarders, staying back.

In January and February one sees a number of unshaven, badly dressed students with dark circles underneath their eyes near the teachers' flats. One of the advantages of having the senior teachers on campus is that the Class XII students can approach them at any civilised hour at a stage when they are pressed for time. Another common sight are the 'Mini School' students. The 'Mini School' programme, involves bringing children from various slums in the city to Modern School in a school bus after school hours. These children are then given lessons by the teachers who take turns to stay back in groups. The students organise sports and activities like painting and sculpture for them. The children stay in school for a few hours, are given tea and biscuits in the evening and sent back in the bus. As darkness sets in, the day scholars leave the campus, the boarders and some of the teachers are served dinner and student activity is confined to the Golden Jubilee Hostel.

At the end of the day, many people ask, what is it that a Modern School education gives you? When one passes out of this institution, one joins the ranks of Air Chief Marshal P.C. Lal, Bharat Ram, Air Chief Marshal S.K. Mehra, Arun Shourie, Dr. Naresh Trehan, Ustad Amjad Ali Khan and Shekhar Kapur, to name a few. Recently when McKinsey International, one of the world's largest management consulting firms, was to announce its CEO, there were two people in the running. Both were Indians and Modernites—Rajat Gupta, who eventually got the job, and Anupam Puri. Yet how much of their success do these people owe to Modern? Is there something Modern has given them, and given the other highly successful alumni?

If one were to ask this question of a Modernite, the first thing they would say, would be 'confidence'. Nothing can illustrate this better than the following anecdote. In the 1930s an Indian students' hockey team was touring Germany. The players were told that when they would be introduced to the German team on the field their hosts would raise their hands and greet them with a 'Heil Hitler'. The Indians were instructed to respond in a similar manner. All the team members complied but one. He was a Modernite by the name of Khushwant Singh.

Modern is a school where I.I.T. toppers win inter-school debates and bunk mathematics classes to play basketball, where national level sportsmen excel in academics and where a student can win an All-India debate a week before his Class XII Boards, get into the Sriram College of Commerce and go on to top the UPSC. One finds that Modernites have distinguished themselves in just about every profession. Their well-rounded education stays with them throughout their lives. A Modernite is invariably exposed to people from every community, region and section of society as the students come from various backgrounds. Most importantly, Modern inculcates in its students a desire to reach the top, no matter what. Second prizes have never been good enough for its students, within school, at inter-school competitions or in life. At the end of the day, Modern is one of the very few institutions that imparts to its students what can truly be called an education, and I thank God I went there.

From the day we enter to the day we leave Modern School, we are a part of an academic, extra-curricular and social world that is ours alone. Modern School students' lives revolve around their school far more than those of other students do around theirs, which is why we miss it so much more. But regardless of who is within those walls, the Modern School tradition to which modern India owes some of its greatest individuals, lives on. On driving past the school, one sometimes yearns, all of a sudden, to be back within those walls of red sandstone with seventy five years of tradition behind them, experiencing once again, what is undoubtedly amongst the finest experiences of one's life.

As a Modernite recently put it:

In laal deewaron ke peechchey
Mera pehla ashiana tha
Mein shair tha mein aashiq tha
Haan woh bhi ek zamana tha.

Let us leave it at that.

A Day In Modern School

Alieda Ali Baig

The alarm clock rings in my ear, and as I wake up and laze in bed, as usual my thoughts turn to school for which I have to get ready soon. But it hasn't always been this way—I haven't always been a seventeen year old, and in class twelve. That realisation comes down on me somewhat heavily. As more than once in the past, a flashback carries me back through the years I have been in Modern School. All those wonderful years. Even as I don the uniform, the seemingly ordinary blue, I remember going with my mother to buy the little dresses we wore in class one—I felt so grown up! And even now, the uniform symbolises so much. It's like the protective all-encompassing arm of the school around me, always there to lean against. In a way it guides me through my day, compelling me to live up to it..... I am startled from my reverie. Gulping down my cup of coffee and ignoring my mother's pleas to eat something, I rush to catch the bus—the first contact of the day with the school.

As I enter the 'hallowed portals' of the school and greet my friends, I can see a new nursery student clinging on to her mother's hand, as she gazes up at the overwhelming red brick structure. I can smile now, but at the back of my mind, I remember the fear and awe I felt as I entered these gates twelve years ago. Everything was so big, and the senior students were almost terrifying in their size and what I imagined to be infinite wisdom!

As I walk further, I am hit by such a strong feeling of freedom, of being alive. Even before classes have begun, the corridors are buzzing with activity. I wish I could put into words the atmosphere of Modern School... . They say that half of what you get out of a day lies in anticipation. So as I enter there is an excitement, a feeling of nervous energy perhaps, as I anticipate no day in Modern School can ever be mundane. Every day is a unique experience. And throughout my day, there is some thing, some sort of an intangible force that keeps that energy there—the energy that never ebbs within these four walls.

We proceed to the field for assembly. I am struck by the fact that in spite of attending so many assemblies, each day still has the power to move me. It's all so familiar on the one hand—the Prefects organising the lines, the school choir setting up the instruments and the long, straight lines of blue.

It can be such a simple, possibly mundane ceremony, yet here it has such a deep, almost spiritual aspect. You realise the unity which can bind a school. The prayer song, the meditation is such an integral part of our morning which clears our mind for the rest of the day. Listening to the meaningful 'thought for the day', announcements of upcoming events and activities, the victories of the school, the sombre voice of the Principal advising us, reprimanding us, inspiring us. I can still feel the patriotism and pride that surged through my blood on Independence day, as the flag unfurled; the laughter and familial warmth, when on children's day the teachers dressed up as students, and acted, danced and sang, pinpointing all our little idiosyncracies.

It's Wednesday and as we go for the inter-House activity, we see the final touches being given by the House incharge before the compere takes over. This kind of exposure is invaluable in giving the students confidence. The opportunity to learn, may be by trial and error, to perform before the entire school, has helped many of us overcome stage fright. I remember the first time I was on stage, I barely reached the mike. In a tremulous voice, I recited the chosen poem (forgot most of the lines, I may add!) but the reassuring and comforting arm of the teacher on my shoulder and the applause that greeted my debut on stage, gave me the confidence to try again.

I can remember so many times practising for our class play, or preparing for an inter-school debate. The teachers and students have always been so encouraging and helpful. This is why, these moments have not just been hard work, but a lot of fun, precious moments I shall always cherish.

We return to class and the periods follow, one after another. Some enjoyable, some taxing—but in all of them the teachers take such trouble to make sure we understand the subject. Going through the rigors of course completion, the heavy load of books, exams—board exams at that looming large on the horizon—we still manage to escape to the library (in search of the latest John Grisham) or to the field for an invigorating game of basketball. In junior classes, report cards were the be-all and end-all of the year, you approached it with such trepidation—as if your little lives depend upon those booklets. Now, while marks and report sheets are still important, what really seems to matter to me, is how much I absorb and learn from it all.

Eleven o' clock—finally. The recess may be short but it is a completely new educative experience in its own right. While I was in class three, the biggest decision was who to share your sandwich with—but now you are lucky if you get even a bite! In a way, recess is the only time of the day when you are not labelled as belonging to any particular class or House. And each day in the midst of tussles over ice creams, mud fights, the noise—there are new situations to face, new friends to make. For all of twenty minutes, the school is transformed into a churning sea of blue, contrasting with the red brick architectural masterpiece that is Modern School.

The rest of the day follows. In between classes, as I talk to my friends I think back to the days when we never had to worry about completing our maths course, or whether or not we'd get into a good college. Back in class six, class twelve was the ultimate—everyone seemed so grown up—but now I'm not half as 'grown up' as I imagined I would be—and sometimes (only sometimes) I do wish I could go back to those easy days, when I never even thought of leaving school.

The bell rings. As we stream out of school and I board the bus to come home, a very disturbing thought crosses my mind. I am reminded that soon I shall walk through this gate for the final time, and into life, all on my own. That thought is terrifying, and I find it hard to fathom my life without school as an anchor. I've had such wonderful, wonderful times here, some of the best times, I think I'll ever have—making such exceptional friends as I have here, and interacting with the superb teachers. But Modern School teaches you so much more—it's given me so many opportunities and such freedom to learn on my own. More than just academics, Modern has given me the strength and confidence to take on the world. It has taught me to be an individual.

Nurturing Values, Crystalising Dreams

S.P. Bakshi

After obtaining post graduate degrees in English and Sociology, I embarked upon my career as a teacher of English in Modern School. The school had assumed a towering status in the country and was a force among the public schools of India. Our NCC contingent used to participate in the All-India Inter-Public Schools NCC contest and year after year, the flag of supremacy was awarded to the Modern School. Based on the inter-school competitions in Delhi, the Delhi Administration used to award the 'Nehru Pataka' to the school which won the highest number of points in inter-school matches. The 'Nehru Pataka' was won every year by Modern School.

I recall having worked with stalwarts like Mr. M.N. Kapur, Mr. Awadh Kishore, Mr. N.K. Bose, Mr. Radhey Mohan Mathur, popularly known as 'Chachaji', Dr. K.D. Bhardwaj, Mr. S.P. Choudhary, Mr. I.B. Dutt, Mr. Vishnu Dutt, Mr. L.N. Khurana, Mr. Ved Vyas, Mr. E.R.R. Menon, Mr. Moolraj Mendiratta, Mr. Jankidas Sharma, Mr. U.S. Nigam and Mr. R. D. Goyal.

Modern School stood for excellence. Lalaji's vision and dream in education was being implemented in this school. Social service, championing the cause of the poor and down-trodden, providing succour to the flood-affected regions of the country, going to orphanages and homes for the blind were important activities of the school. A feeling was instilled in the minds of students that if they were comparatively comfortable and rich in life, they owed a debt to society.

The school community then was twenty-nine or thirty teachers and five hundred students and the school functioned from 8 a.m. to 4 p.m. Unofficially, we would invariably work till late in the evening, on *Sandesh* or *Adarsh*, or preparing a House function, a debate or declamation contest, or games and sports, or simply detention of students by a Housemaster, or inter-House matches or preparation for inter-school contests. The school was virtually 'on' from morning till night.

In the year 1970-71, I was awarded a Fulbright scholarship to teach English in a high school in the USA. This took me to a small town called Fort Wayne in Indiana. There were three hundred teachers in the school with three thousand kids. The school was known for football, wrestling and basketball. Before the expiry of my tenure in the school, the Principal Dr. Bill Anthis persuaded me to continue. He wanted to take advantage of my experience in Modern School. I knew I had made a commitment to Modern School before leaving for the States, so I faithfully reported back for duty.

The school had just concluded its Golden Jubilee, Sir Shankarlal Hall had been built and also the boarding house of the school which was named the Golden Jubilee Hostel. With the addition of the Shankarlal Hall, we had now a bigger laboratory available for further experimentation in cultural and co-curricular activities which were an integral part of the general education imparted in the school. I remember Mr. Ved Vyas developed a new form in the field of performing arts called Rupak which we staged in the presence of the Prime Minister of India, Mrs. Indira Gandhi.

The seminary provides a child with an environment that is homely; the child doesn't feel homesick as the teachers stand as another set of parents. Every school imparts education and good teachers are everywhere but when it comes to Modern, it is the all-round development and refinement of the child's personality. This I feel has been the distinguishing feature of Modern School.

I left Modern School in the year 1977 to take charge of the Army Public School at Dhaula Kuan. The success that I achieved in that school was essentially due to my grounding and training in Modern School, where I had become a member of a team which was entrusted with the responsibility of nurturing, and implementing values of secularism, humanism, catholicity of temper and ability to face crises. In 1982, I was invited to rejoin Modern. I realised that Modern had passed through a bad patch and I accepted the challenge. I found this vast laboratory, spread over twenty-five acres very inviting and hospitable.

In 1982, at a meeting with the school Prefects in my office, it was decided that we should organise a Blood Donation Camp in the school. The response from the student community was phenomenal. The Blood Donation Camp became an annual feature of the school calendar and year after year more and more students volunteered and spontaneously donated blood. The Director of the Red Cross felt that this was one of the most successful camps in his entire career.

With the construction of the Sobha Singh Block which is a classroom complex, the need for additional class rooms had been met but in order to enrich the school further, an Olympic size swimming pool and standard squash courts were added. Over the years, we have been feeling that our laboratories and computer rooms, though well-equipped, do not measure up to our ambitious plans. We thought that the Platinum Jubilee Year was most appropriate for the construction of a building complex which will house modern laboratories, lecture demonstration rooms and a mini multi-purpose hall for audio-visual facilities and lectures by visiting luminaries from time to time. As we see this building complex taking shape, our dream over the years, seems to be crystallizing.

The presentation of *Jesus Christ Superstar* at the Siri Fort Auditorium proved eventually that Modern is capable of accepting any challenge. It was felt that we were good in Hindi plays and ballets, but once we have performed an opera, most of the people conceded our talent in an entirely different type of theatre. When I went on the stage after the musical and embraced Rohan Aggarwal who had played Jesus Christ, we both became emotional and his eyes welled up with tears. There were tears in my eyes as well—the tears of joy, ecstasy, exuberance, of having achieved what at one stage seemed highly unattainable, almost impossible.

Most people were sceptical when Lala Raghubir Singh, the founder, expressed a desire to build a modern school along the lines of Eton, and Harrow. But being a man of integrity reaction, Lalaji, finally gave shape to his idea in 1920 at Daryaganj. The idea was mooted in him by Gandhiji, when the Mahatma visited the Bishop Cotton School in 1915 and liked everything but the 'missionary tag' attached to it. Few people know that Modern School was started at the behest of the Father of the Nation.

There is hardly any university in the world where our old students are not only studying but are fairly conspicuous by their presence and achievements. In 1994 Pavinder Singh was invited by Harvard University with a full scholarship. It was a treat to read the invitation—it was so polite and persuasive. Srivatsa Krishna stood first in the All-India Administrative Services Examination in 1994; Rajat Gupta was the first Indian to head Mckinsey, the biggest financial giant of the world. I feel proud of some of the top scientists, doctors, journalists, social workers, film stars, builders, architects, civil services officers, defence officers in the country and various parts of the world who are Modernites.

Over the years, Modern School has become a part and parcel of my living and thinking. The students of this great institution, with their attainments and achievements, are eloquent testimony to the realisation of Lalaji's dream of an independent India.

Vision For The 21st Century: Vasant Vihar Modern School

K.J. Vari

Modern School was set up seventy-five years ago with a specific mission. This mission was to impart education that would meet the challenges that lay ahead of students as responsible citizens of this land.

From its inception, the school has turned out an impressive array of leaders in every field who have influenced the course of events by their foresight and contribution. Society still looks up to the school to continue doing this. Our country is caught up with the phenomenal progress that is taking place in all walks of life. Leaders of sound moral and administrative stature, who are wise managers of change, are the need of the hour. Going by the pace of progress and the rate of change we are witnessing now, one is overwhelmed to conjecture its scale and pace in the 21st century.

Therefore, to my mind, the school should strive to address the above need with renewed vigour. We should tap everything modern educational technology can offer, keeping clearly focussed in our minds the caution given by the Father of the Nation during a visit to the School on 13 January 1935. 'The scholars—young men and women—might lose much, if the *ancient* would disappear in the onrush of the *modern*.' This implies that while we keep up with progress we have to root ourselves firmly in the rich heritage that has been handed down to us by our forefathers. This is becoming a daunting task.

The phenomenal expansion in the body of knowledge in all fields particularly in the scientific and technological areas, and the explosion in the field of communication, are placing unprecedented demands on the child. The 'rush of the modern' seems to engulf him. At the early stages of the school, great emphasis was laid on learning by doing. Gradually there was a withdrawal to the class room, the chalk and the board. This has to be reversed if we are to live by the agenda set by the founder, who envisaged education to mean the careful all-round development of the student by life-experiences, rather than turning him into a storehouse of information.

In order to reverse this disturbing trend, the only option before us is to tap the excellent educational technology now available. While doing so, bold departures will have to be made in the process and the methods of instruction. At present the teaching faculty is under-prepared to take this initiative though there are a few who venture into innovative areas. Hence there has to be a massive empowerment programme for teachers to equip them with the ability to make use of all that is offered by modern education technology. This is particularly important when it comes to making computer-assisted learning possible with the aid of software that is becoming available in every subject. The dependence on modern technology must not be at the cost of relying on the immediate environment and day to day life-experiences to generate creative learning in children.

During the first years of Modern School, a curriculum was created to impart education, embodying the philosophy of the founder. Now we have to restructure the existing curriculum and go back to the basics. There are serious obstacles in effecting this. Connected with this is the fact that students have to come from far-flung areas, taking hours to commute to school. One sure solution to this is to turn Modern School into a neighbourhood school and once more to make it a full-day school. While making it a full-day school there must be enough infrastructure and programmes to cater to the needs of students in the various age groups. In addition to learning subjects through creative and project-based methods with emphasis on hands-on learning, there should be adequate time for reinforcement of learning through supervised homework and self-revision. There should also be specialized programmes for empowering the weak and the gifted students.

One of the areas that will require urgent attention is career guidance and preparation for competitive examinations. With the remarkable opening up of employment opportunities in areas of specialization hitherto unheard of, career guidance and preparation for specialization requires scientific handling. This will be more so in the 21st century. Japanese students often spend a fourteenth year at school precisely for this purpose. The scientific handling of career guidance should make it possible to branch out from career-counselling workshops and seminars to shop floor hands-on exposure for familiarization in industries, firms and institutions. Only this can ensure the correct choice of a career which will match the strengths of a student. This important task is now rather feebly addressed, often leaving it to the choice and wishes of parents. The school library should be provided with adequate and uptodate informative literature on career areas and the students should be assisted with carrying out guided research on careers.

While specialization in a particular area is a must in preparing for a career, one important aspect should be kept in mind. In every field of specialization there is and will be, in a more pronounced manner, interdependence on various other fields. Hence students have to be well-informed in a variety of other areas. In order to facilitate proper and in-depth specialization as well as to acquire sufficient familiarity with related fields, a well equipped library is a *sine qua non*. Such a library must have all kinds of facilities that are found in the libraries of good institutions anywhere in the world. The library must become central to the acquisition of knowledge and specialization. The number and the range of books and reference materials should be adequate and constantly updated. Language teaching should be made to include guiding the students in the use of the library books as a powerful tool of research and self learning. With the tremendous media explosion, there is a marked and dangerous decline in the reading habits of young people. This explosion will increase at an unprecedented scale in the 21st century. The library should be available for use to students, especially of the senior classes, for as long a period of the day as possible, even outside the normal working hours. The implementation of a full-day school and the adoption of the neighbourhood school concept will enhance the possibility of full and meaningful utilization of the library.

One major area of frustration and trauma for the students is the burden placed on them by an outmoded curriculum and highly questionable form of evaluation. Even the CBSE (Central Board of Secondary Education) to which the school is affiliated recognises this. As the nation marches towards the 21st century, we should think in terms of affiliation to more than one affiliating body in India and abroad so that our students can be given opportunities to take advantage of the globalisation of education made possible by the communication explosion which has led to global networking.

Compared to most other schools, we are fortunate to have considerable space for sports available to us. However, the fields are not sufficient to cater to the two thousand odd students in the school. Yet provision of more infrastructure and careful management of the available space and facilities should improve matters a great deal. As in the early years of Modern School, an all-out effort should be made to provide adequate physical training to students each week, involving each and every one.

The relentless onrush of the 'modern' is now more than ever threatening to flood out the 'ancient' just as Mahatma Gandhi warned Modern School. From the age of deprivation our country is passing precipitously to the age of acquisition. Materialism has taken hold of every one. The traditional values handed down to us through the ages are being discounted, bringing about a gradual spiritual bankruptcy. This danger is going to be aggravated in the 21st century. Professions are chosen solely on the basis of material returns. The disastrous effect of materialism on advanced societies is there for all to see. The school has to make a determined, sustained and all-out effort to counter this if we are to survive as a society with its rich heritage of tradition and time-tested values.

The gradual breaking up of the joint family system, which used to be the conduit for handing down the traditional values, and the evolution of unclear families, where parent-children interaction is considerably reduced in quantum and quality, have scaled down the role that traditional Indian families played in value education. Parents themselves are caught off-guard, not knowing how to cope with the fast changing social and economic scenario and keeping their children rooted in our traditional values. This places additional responsibility on the school to play a more dynamic and vital role.

Society is not what it was when the school was founded in 1920. Vast changes have taken place even during twenty years that this campus has been in existence. Vaster and unimaginable may be the changes which are likely to take place in the 21st century. Hence, we have to address ourselves to an increasing need to impart education for social responsibility. On the one hand, it has to do with the individual and the family in society and on the other hand it has to do with the individual and society in relation to the environment. Age-old social structures like the family system are crumbling with the arrival of the live-in system. Like the recent media invasion from the skies, these and other structural changes will invade our society in a big way in the next decades and we must be prepared to deal with it while educating our students.

Serious efforts must be made to impart environmental education if we are to survive on this planet. Since the industrial revolution, in gradual escalation, there has been an unmindful degradation and exploitation of the environment. In the name of progress, the economic balance is being precariously threatened, striking at the very foundation of the survival of the human race and all life forms. It is going to be a far more difficult task in the future to rein in the march of progress at the cost of the environment. Our students are going to be the future leaders of the country and they should be made to realise this responsibility.

Those who join the field of school education are increasingly losing sight of the awesome responsibility that they are taking upon themselves. There are a host of reasons for this, for which our society as a whole is responsible. But it is imperative for teachers to acquire the vision, mission and dedication as 'gurus'. We should try in our schools to create conditions to re-establish the *guru-shishya-parampara*. On the surface this may seem impossible. The major reasons for the breakdown of this relationship are the problem of the numbers in classes that teachers have to deal with, the lack of time and the tremendous day-to-day pressures that teachers confront. An all-out effort must be made to remedy these, so that education in our school becomes a noble profession, nobly practised. To achieve this we should do everything in our power to attract the best talent to our school and be prepared to pay the price for it. Education is communication and communication is education. To achieve total communication is no mean task even within a congenial environment. It is essential for the school to build on the existing modes and channels of communication and remove obstacles that now exist.

The aims and objectives set forth by Lala Raghubir Singh and the basic approach and methodology are equally relevant but the educational scenario today is so transformed that it is almost unrecognizable. But with the changes that have occurred through the march of time, Modern School has all along modified its approach and strategy. What the 21st century has in store for us and mankind in general is almost impossible to imagine. I have no doubt in my mind that Modern School will always face up to the challenges as it has in the past and will always be a temple of learning, imparting education for a meaningful life.

Vision For The 21st Century: Raghubir Singh Junior Modern School

Geeta Dudeja

The primary goal of education, as envisioned by Lala Raghubir Singh in 1920, was to help a child grow into a rounded and well-balanced personality, well-integrated in society and a citizen that the country could be proud of. That he would be educated and knowledgeable was of secondary importance. The universal application and timelessness of this perception of true education is as valid today as it has been over the past seventy-five years. How this goal is to be achieved and adapted according to the requirements of the day, is what needs the close attention of educationists in the country.

Modern School, the trail-blazer in achieving this goal, has been steadily reflecting and reaffirming, over the years, the continued applicability and inherent flexibility of Lalaji's basic vision.

In the 1920s, when the need of the hour was to uplift the spirit of the Indians under the British Raj, that is what the school achieved. Children were made to feel proud of being Indians. Both boys and girls were given equal opportunities in all fields. In the late 1940s, when the need of the hour was patriotic fervour, that is what was created in the children. They were made to feel equal to the ruling community. Ram Mohan Gandhi, an old student, spoke about the school at a recent M.N. Kapur Memorial lecture. Referring to the looting and bloodshed of 1947, he felt that Modern School was an oasis where all religions were respected and the children felt secure and protected from feelings of communal bitterness. And, indeed, that is the strength of the school. Today, the need is to remove economic disparities, class and caste distinctions and behavioral aberrations like the drug menace. Tomorrow, when the need of the twenty-first century will be to provide broad-based knowledge, relevant to the times, the school will adapt itself to these requirements of the future. The school will not only enable the students to understand and integrate themselves into the technologically and economically expanding world, without losing their national, cultural and individual identities, but also help them to utilise every possible facility and talent available.

The function of the Junior School is most important in the formation of the child's character. Raghubir Singh Junior Modern School has been preparing young children to meet the challenges of an adult world with confidence and integrity, providing a basic foundation that allows a beautiful structure to be constructed. This being so, our vision for the next century remains unchanged. The areas which will need some modification are:

Readapt the equipment of the children with modern technology and advanced scientific techniques to help them face the competitive challenges of the twenty-first century.

Focus on general awareness of environment and conservation of natural resources.

Re-organise time-table and activities so as to free the school premises for another 'shift', with greater emphasis on the weaker sections of society.

Tap and pool all the talent available among parents, assistant teachers, and senior students, to help in educating the less fortunate.

In my view, the ways in which these objectives may be fulfilled are:

—In a century of extreme competition in academics and vocations, children from the primary school must be encouraged to handle computers freely. Greater emphasis must be laid on assessing a child's capabilities and reinforcing its natural strengths. This enables a child to choose a career with ease and confidence. Simultaneously, parents must be educated to consider all vocations at par, without hankering for pure academics for their children.

—Projects to utilise the school premises in the afternoons must be drawn without any income-based segregation of children.

—Students of Class V should be encouraged to interact with the younger, less fortunate children, whenever time permits, and parents with spare time should be encouraged to help on a day-to-day basis, in the fields of their specialisation.

To achieve these goals, the school will need extensive funds to provide for computers and for 'centres' of science (including conservation of environment), languages and activities like art, pottery and carpentry. The plans for these projects could be developed along the lines of a corporate enterprise wherein the public can invest and contribute towards the fulfilment of this need.

Above all, the vision of Lala Raghubir Singh should be held in constant focus. The changes should not, at any cost, bury under the layers of scientific and high-tech life-styles ahead of us the cultural and aesthetic values inherent in the education system of the Modern School.

A Vision For Modern School

Ashok Pratap Singh

Modern School was founded with the aims and objectives of creating leaders. The founder perceived that in the years to come people would be needed to administer the country through its major transitory phase. Transition, change and growth are unending. As transportation and communications become more efficient and more sophisticated, the country becomes an integral part of the world. Our need to create leaders continues unabated. Leaders who will help integrate India with the world.

In this holistic sense the vision over the last seventy-five years has remained constant.

A vision has a very short life if steps are not taken to convert it to a meaningful reality.

What must Modern School do?

We must strive for excellence in academics.
We must strive for excellence in sports.
We must strive for excellence in the fine and performing arts.
We must provide facilities for new and emergent fields of study.
We must provide flexibility of programmes and curriculum to enable every student to develop his full potential.
We must look beyond ourselves to integrate our education with the best in the world.
We must provide the best facilities to the teachers, who are the chief implementors of this vision.

This striving for excellence would provide the basis for encouraging the Modern School students—

To emerge into life with confidence but without over-confidence.
To develop individuality without forgetting the importance of team work.
To develop into individuals of intelligence, compassion and physical fitness.

To help and support those who are in need without losing dignity or sense of compassion.
To be pace-setters with pride in themselves and their country in whatever field they choose, wherever in the world they may be.
And most importantly to recognise that the greatest success lies in the ability to live with humility and to shun arrogance.

For all this and much more, the vision of Modern School must be to dream and to bring those dreams to earth, but never to be left behind because one did not dream enough.

To continue to look outwards—beyond the horizon, beyond the dimension of time, without losing sight of one's own limitations and the day-to-day realities of life.

Appendices

Appendix I

Rudra Prize

The Rudra Prize was instituted in 1928 and named after Sushil Kumar Rudra, one of the school's members, and the Principal of St. Stephen's College, Delhi.

It was awarded to the best all-round student for character combined with learning. The criteria as stated in *A Successful Experiment in Education* (1947) were as follows:

Academic achievement; originality—music, art, literature and science; helpfulness; sense of responsibility; leadership; clean living; respect towards elders, teachers, fellow students; perseverance; personality; loyalty; care of health; skill and regularity in games; sportsmanship; scouting; manual or hand-work; hobbies—utilization of leisure.

1928 — Bhagwant Singh
1929 — Pritam Singh
1930 — Pratap Singh
1931 — Bharat Ram, Pritam Sen
1932 — Narendra Singh
1935 — Chand Prakash
1937 — Daljit Singh, Bishamber Dayal
1938 — Rabindra Nath Bose
1939 — Raghuraj Bahadur
1940 — Suresh Narain
1941 — Rathindra Nath Bose
1944 — Yogendra Kumar Barman
1946 — Shivraj Kishore
1948 — Satish Mohan
1949 — Khalari Lal, Prabhat Chandra
1951 — Purshotam Ghei
1953 — Shashi Prakash Puri
1954 — Vinod Dikshit, Ramchandra Gandhi
1955 — Kuldip Sahdev
1956 — Surya Kumar, Mahinder Kumar
1957 — Arvind Varma, Nareshwar Dayal
1958 — Ina Dhanda, Ajit Kishore
1959 — Geeta Kapur, Neera Kukreja
1960 — Manmohan Mehra
1961 — Anwar Abbas
1962 — Purnima Mehta, Rajat K. Narain
1963 — Vijay Bedi, Chandana Singh
1964 — Kanchan Mala, Madhusudan, Santosh Mathur
1965 — Ravi Narayan, Hemant Luthra
1966 — Rajat Gupta, Manmohan Singh
1967 — Kapil Malhotra
1968 — Ravindra Bhatt
1969 — Shyam Kamath, Jayant Prasad
1970 — Samir Mathur
1971 — Rajesh Nandan Pande, Rahul Sud
1972 — Rajeev Bhargav
1973 — Richa Vyas, Nivedita Sengupta
1974 — Sanjeev Manchanda, Kanwaljit Singh Goindi

1976 — Arvind Datt, Neera Nath
1977 — Maitreyee Barthakur
1979 — Vivek Rampal
1980 — Ashwajit Singh
1982 — Abhinav Chaturvedi
1983 — Vandana Mittal, Aseem Prakash
1984 — Vikas Jalan
1985 — Ajay Bijli, Sidhartha Kaul
1986 — Ravin Sachdeva, Gaurav Mehra
1987 — Sonam Bakhshi
1988 — Tanusha Mittal
1989 — Anjali Jain
1990 — Bhanu Baweja
1991 — Parul Sharma
1992 — Bansuri Taneja
1993 — Bulbul Khera, Ishita Ganguli
1994 — Pavninder Singh
2000 — Raghav Kapur
2001 — Ashish Jain
2002 — Tanya Aggarwal
2003 — Shloka Vaidialingam
2004 — Neeta Bala
2005 — Divya Jain
2006 — Sahil Rajvansh
2007 — Nandini Singh
2008 — Pallavi Jain, Nimit Jain, Gaurav Sabharwal
2009 — Aakarshan Kumar
2010 — Sidhant Kumar Marwah
2011 — Devika Mittal, Shreya Ghei
2012 — Dhruv C. Aggarwal
2013 — Pranay Lekhi
2014 — Dhruv Pargai
2015 — Sandhini Agarwal
2016 — Parth Bhatia
2017 — Prateek Kher & Neelesh Pandey
2018 — Aatmik Gupta
2019 — Abhinav Agarwal

Appendix II

Roll of Honour

Major S.K. Dang lost his life at Tenga Valley in 1962 during the war with China. He completed his studies at Modern School in 1949.

Flt. Lt. Satish Bharadwaj of Indian Air Force relinquished life on September 1, 1965 during the Indo-Pak conflict. He joined Modern School in 1952 and completed his studies in 1957. Always a braveheart, he died fighting for his country.

Capt. Kiran Seth died a hero's death in the Sialkot Sector during the Indo-Pak War. During his ten years' stay at Modern School he excelled in games and sports and won the Best Cadet Trophy in 1958 in the NCC. The Kiran Seth Memorial prize has been named after this young versatile hero.

Flt. Lt. Tanmaya Singh Dandass joined Modern School in 1951 and passed out in 1962. He was an outstanding athlete and won State colours. He was declared best NCC Cadet for two consecutive years. He died in action in the Indo-Pak War at the age of 25.

Born in 1964, **Col. Sonam Wangchuk** is a native of Khakshal, part of Leh, in the Ladakh region of the Indian state of Jammu and Kashmir. He had his education at Sacred Heart High School, Dharamshala and Modern School Barakhamba Road. He displayed bravery and gallantry of the highest order in the presence of enemy fire and in extreme climatic conditions in the glaciated area of Chorbatla axis in the Batalik Sector and cleared the axis up to the Line of Control of all enemy intrusions at great risk to his life and was awarded Mahavir Chakra in 1999.

Contributors

Khushwant Singh was a student of Modern School from 1920 to 1930. He was awarded Padma Bhushan in 1974 and Padma Vibhushan in 2007.

Syeda Saiyidain Hameed was a student of Modern School from 1955 to 1959. She is an educationist, writer and former member of the Planning Commission of India. She was awarded Padma Shri in 2007.

Reverend C.F. Andrews was a colleague and friend of Mahatma Gandhi, first in South Africa, then in India. He was also associated with Gurudev Rabindranath Tagore. He was Professor at St. Stephen's College, Delhi.

Lala Raghubir Singh was the founder of Modern School and the first Secretary of its Board of Trustees. He was educated in Delhi and England. He died in 1959.

Kamala Bose was appointed the first Principal of Modern School in 1920. She was born and educated in Calcutta. She served as an inspectress of schools in Calcutta and the Principal of various schools in Calcutta and Gopalgunj. For twenty-seven years she headed the Modern School. She died in 1948.

M.N. Kapur was the second Principal of Modern School from 1947 to 1977. He was educated in Lahore and in London. Before joining Modern, he taught at Mayo College, Ajmer. He died in 1994.

Amrita Kapur was associated for thirty years with the educational experiments of her husband M.N. Kapur at Modern School. She was educated in Lahore. She taught at Lahore, Ajmer and Modern School.

Bhagwant Singh, the eldest son of Sardar Sobha Singh, was the first Modernite, from 1920 to 1928. He was a member of the Board of Trustees from 1997-2000.

Bharat Ram was a student of Modern School from 1924 to 1931. He was a leading industrialist of the country and was awarded Padma Bhushan in 1972.

Ved Vyas taught at Modern School from 1949 to 1986—for the last ten years he was the Principal of Modern School, Vasant Vihar. Besides being an educationist, he was a poet, writer, actor, theatre director and filmmaker of childrens' films for educational television.

Madhusudan Panikkar was a student of Modern School from 1929 to 1938. He studied at Delhi and at Cambridge, England. He was a journalist and author, who has written on African history and politics and on West Asia.

Ketaki Sood was a student of Modern School from 1945 to 1957. She is an interior designer by profession and has studied in Delhi and London. A member of the Board of Trustees since 1975, she is its current President since 2018.

Shobha Deepak Singh was a student of Modern School from 1957 to 1960. She is the Director of Shriram Bharatiya Kala Kendra, specializing in costume design, staging and scripting productions. She was awarded Padma Shri in 1999.

Ashok Dhawan was a student of Modern School from 1946 to 1958. He is an architect, who after having spent twenty years studying and working in the USA, Iran, Saudi Arabia and Kuwait, has returned to India and is now practising in Delhi.

Geeta Kapur was a student of Modern School from 1947 to 1959. She studied art in New York and London. A freelance critic living in Delhi, she has published widely on art, film and cultural studies. She was awarded Padma Shri in 2009.

Nilima Dhanda Sheikh was a student of Modern School from 1950 to 1962. She has studied art in Baroda and has widely exhibited in India and abroad. She lives in Baroda.

Amjad Ali Khan was a student of Modern School from 1958 to 1963. A maestro of sarod, he is among the most accomplished musicians of the world. He was awarded Padma Vibhushan in 2001.

Anuradha Kapur was a student of Modern School from 1955 to 1967. She studied drama and theatre at the Leeds University. As a theatre director she has produced plays in Delhi and London. She has taught at the National School of Drama, Delhi for over three decades and was its director for 6 years.

Anwar Abbas was a student of Modern School from 1956 to 1961. He is a prominent journalist and the Director of the Habib Public School. He lives in Karachi, Pakistan.

Pavan Ahluwalia was a student of Modern School from 1988-1995. He studied humanities and was the Academic Prefect of the school. He studied at Princeton University, USA.

Alieda Ali Baig was student of Modern School, Vasant Vihar.

S.P. Bakshi was the Principal of Modern School Barakhamba Road from 1982-1996. He was educated in Delhi and USA. He is associated with several educational and professional bodies including the National Council of Teacher Education and the Central Board of Secondary Education.

K.J. Vari joined Modern School, Vasant Vihar in 1982 and was its Principal from 1986-2000. He was educated in Bangalore where he studied Philosophy, Linguistics and English. He is an accomplished artist in Karnataka and Western vocal and instrumental music.

Geeta Dudeja joined the Raghubir Singh Junior Modern School as a teacher in 1964 and took over as its Headmistress in 1991. She is the author of several books for children in Hindi and English.

Ashok Pratap Singh, grandson of Lala Raghubir Singh, was a student of Modern School from 1949 to 1952. He was also educated in Dehradun and in Cambridge, England, where he read natural sciences. He has been the Honorary Secretary of the Board of Trustees since 1982 and President from 2010-2018.

O.P. Sharma, a science graduate turned photographer, joined Modern School in 1960. A winner of over four hundred awards, both national and international, he has exhibited in India and abroad. He is the Honorary General-Secretary of the India International Photographic Council, a Fellow of the Royal Photographic Society of England, the Photographic Society of the USA and other international bodies.

To all those who cherish their memories of Modern School

Lala Raghubir Singh, 1895-1959

Board of Trustees—2020

Mrs. Ketaki Sood,
Hon. President,
Board of Trustees

Mr. Ashok Pratap Singh,
Member,
Board of Trustees

Mrs. Anuradha Singh,
Member, Board of Trustees &
Chairperson, RS Jr Modern
School, Humayun Road

Mrs. Ambika Pant,
Hon. Secretary,
Board of Trustees

Mrs. Mira Pradeep Singh,
Hon. Treasurer,
Board of Trustees

Dr. Geetanjali Chanda,
Member,
Board of Trustees

Mr. Preminder Singh,
Member,
Board of Trustees

Mr. Sunder Hemrajani,
Term-Trustee,
Board of Trustees

Col. Vijay Chadda,
Chairman, Modern School,
Barakhamba Road

Mr. TCA Rangachari,
Chairman,
Modern School,
Vasant Vihar

Dr. Vijay Datta,
Principal,
Modern School,
Barakhamba Road

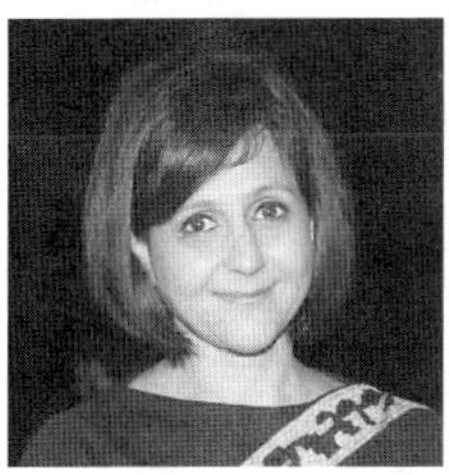

Mrs. Meenakshi Sahni,
Principal,
Modern School,
Vasant Vihar

Mrs. Manju Rajput,
Principal,
RS Jr Modern School,
Humayun Road

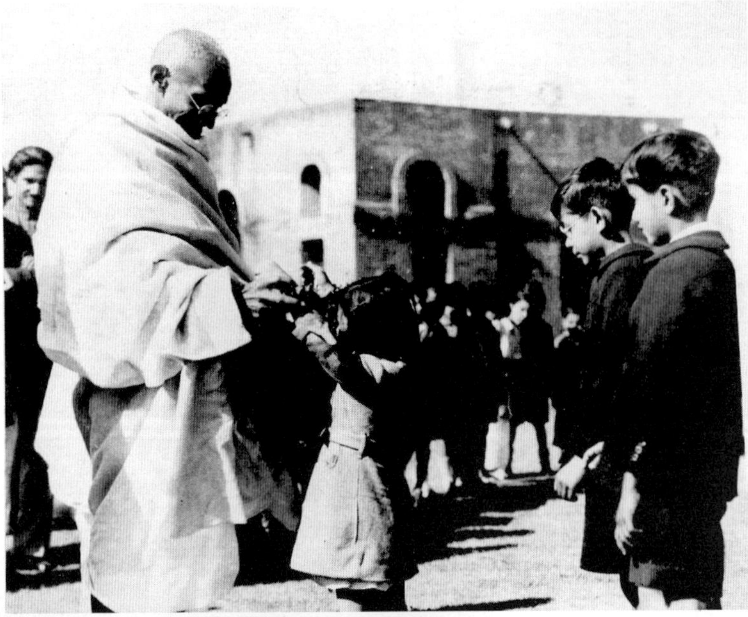

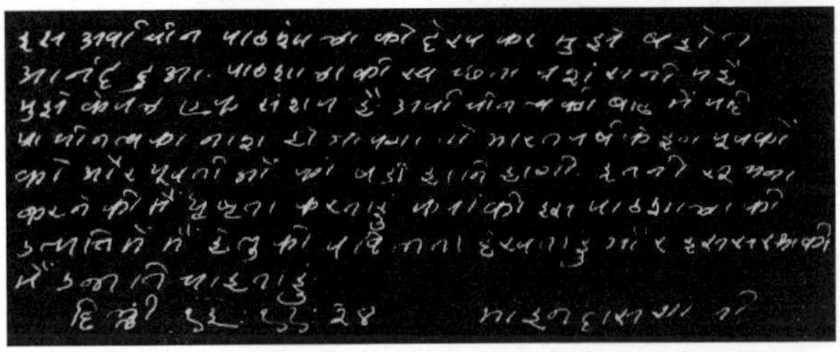

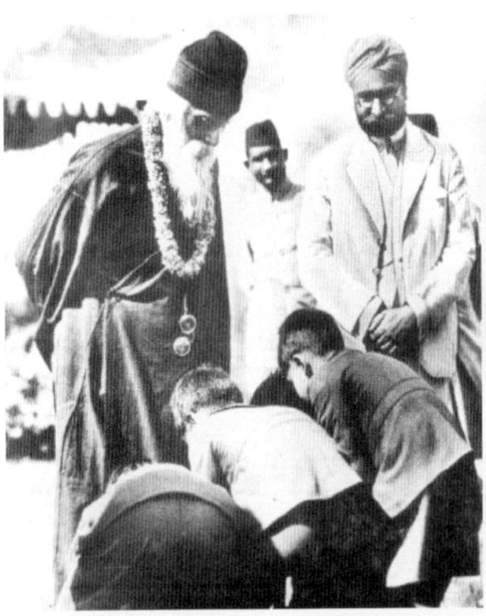

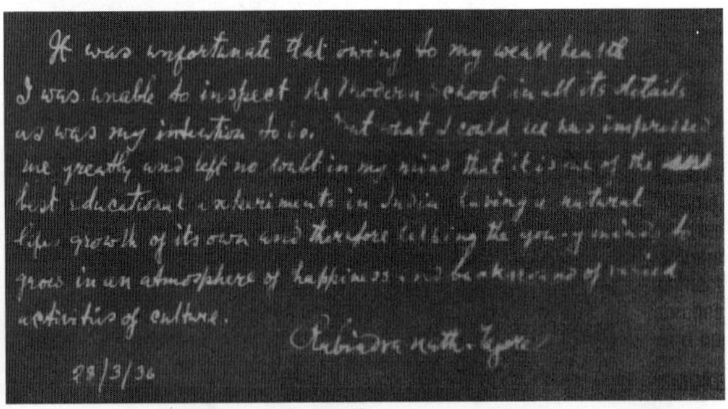

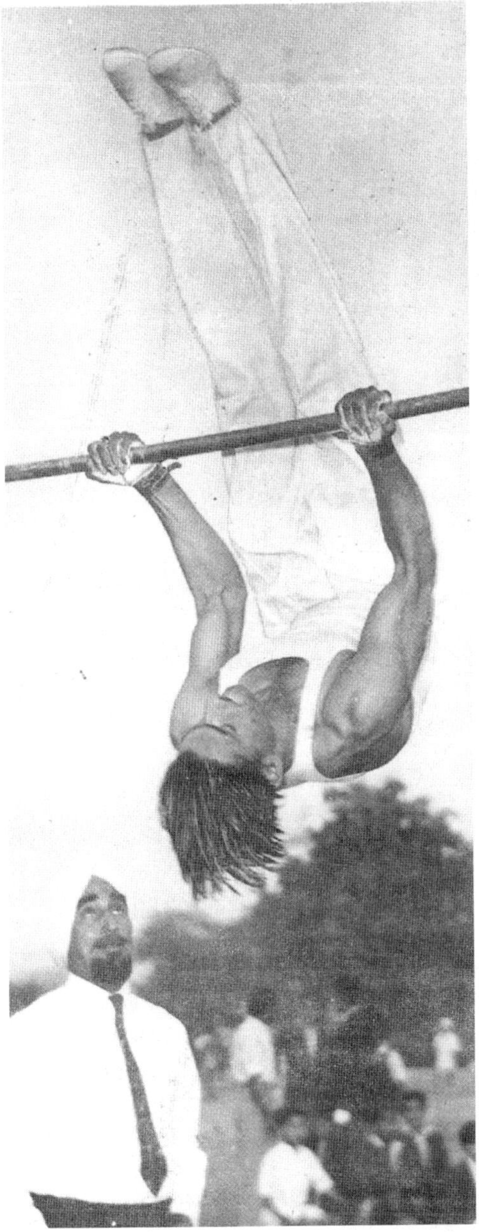

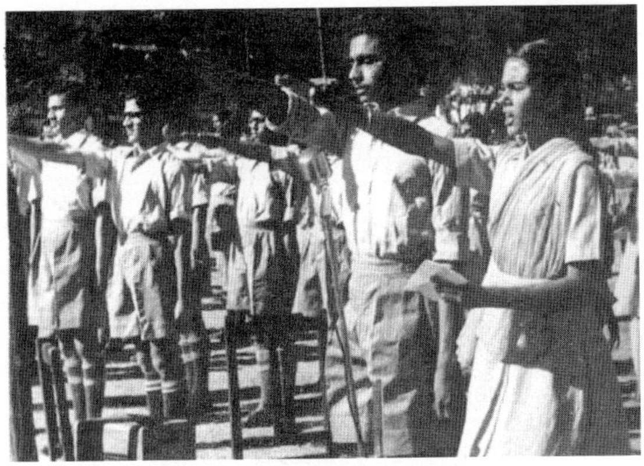

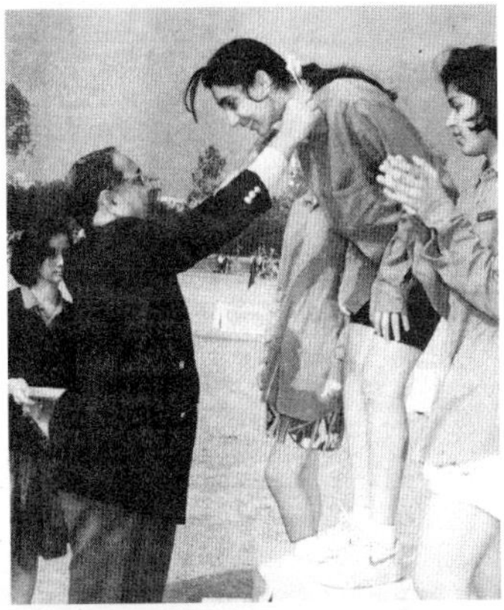

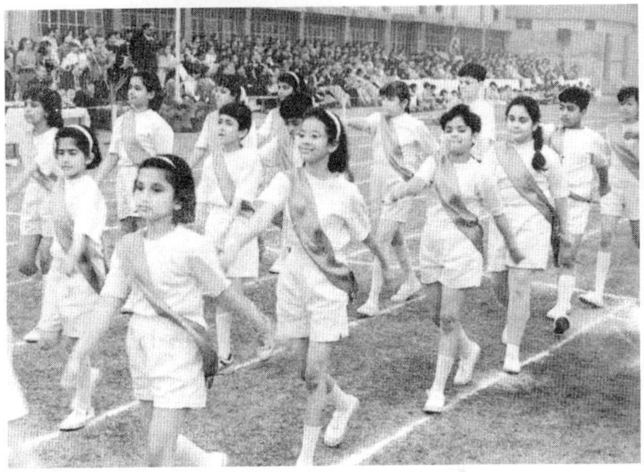

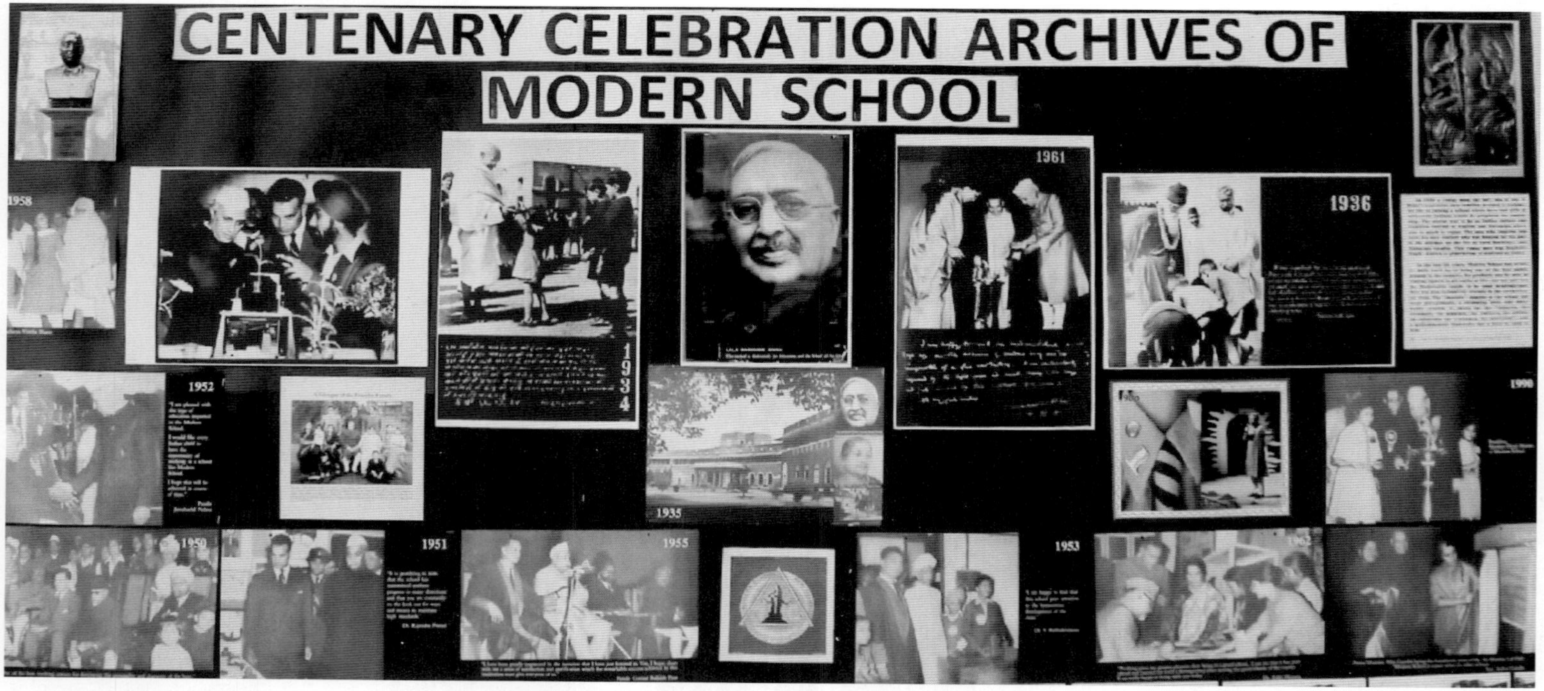

